The School Leader's Guide to Formative Assessment

Todd Stanley & Dr. Jana Alig

Using Data to Improve Student and Teacher Achievement

Routledge
Taylor & Francis Group

NEW YORK AND LONDON

First published 2014
by Routledge
711 Third Avenue, New York, NY 10017

Simultaneously published in the UK
by Routledge
2 Park Square, Milton Park, Abingdon, Oxon OX14 4RN

Routledge is an imprint of the Taylor & Francis Group, an informa business

Library of Congress Cataloging-in-Publication Data

Stanley, Todd.
  The school leader's guide to formative assessment : using data to improve
student and teacher achievement / by Todd Stanley and Dr. Jana Alig.
     pages cm
1. Educational tests and measurements. 2. Academic achievement—Testing.
3. Examinations—Interpretation. I. Title.
  LB3051.S796 2013
  371.26--dc23   2013004475

ISBN: 978-1-59667-246-8 (pbk)

Typeset in Palatino
by Rick Soldin

Cover designer: Dave Strauss, 3FoldDesign

Printed and bound in the United States of America by Publishers Graphics,
LLC on sustainably sourced paper.

Other Eye On Education Books
Available from Routledge

Critical Thinking and Formative Assessments:
Increasing the Rigor in Your Classroom
Betsy Moore and Todd Stanley

Short Cycle Assessment: Improving Student Achievement
Through Formative Assessment
Susan Lang, Todd Stanley, and Betsy Moore

Formative Assessments in a Professional
Learning Community
Todd Stanley and Betsy Moore

Assessing Critical Thinking in Elementary Schools:
Meeting the Common Core
Assessing Critical Thinking in Middle and High Schools:
Meeting the Common Core
Rebecca Stobaugh

Using Formative Assessment to Drive Mathematics
Instruction in Grades PreK–2
Using Formative Assessment to Drive Mathematics
Instruction in Grades 3–5
Christine Oberdorf and Jennifer Taylor-Cox

Test Less, Assess More: A K–8 Guide to
Formative Assessment
Leighangela Brady and Lisa McColl

I Have the Data … Now What? Analyzing Data and
Making Instructional Changes
Betsy Moore

Data, Data Everywhere: Bringing All the Data Together for
Continuous School Improvement
Victoria L. Bernhardt

RTI and CSI: Using Data, Vision, and Leadership to Design,
Implement, and Evaluate a Schoolwide Prevention System
Victoria L. Bernhardt and Connie L. Hébert

Dedication

This book is dedicated to Betsy Moore. We both had the privilege of working with Betsy in the LCAP program through the Ohio Coalition of Essential Schools. Betsy was a wonderful colleague and friend who was always quick to remind us to do "what was best for kids." She spent many years in the classroom changing the lives of children and many years training teacher-leaders to help them become better educators. She co-wrote three books with Todd Stanley for Eye On Education: *Short-Cycle Assessment: Improving Student Achievement through Formative Assessment*, *Critical Thinking and Formative Assessments: Increasing the Rigor in Your Classroom*, and *Formative Assessments in a Professional Learning Community*. She also authored her own book, *I Have the Data … Now What? Analyzing Data and Making Instructional Changes*. Betsy was taken from us too soon in 2011, but we are eternally grateful for the time spent with her.

Contents

About the Authors vii

Pre-Assessment: Formative Assessment #1 ix

Introduction: Using Formative Assessment to
Transform Your School 1

Chapter 1 • Why Use Formative Assessments? 5
Rethinking Assessments 5
The Pudding 7
The Advantages of Formative Assessments 11

Chapter 2 • How You Can Use Formative Assessment 15
What Is a Formative Assessment? 15
What Are Common Formative Assessments? 16
What Are the Advantages of Common
Formative Assessments? 18
When Do You Use Formative Assessments? 20

Chapter 3 • Developing Valid and Reliable Assessments 25
The SCORE Process 28

Chapter 4 • Creating the Assessment Environment 43
Conveying the Message 45
To Review or Not to Review? 46
Creating the Environment 47
Mimicking the State Assessment Schedule 48

Chapter 5 • Organizing and Using Data Effectively 53

Organizing the Data 55

Improving Student Achievement 64

Using Data to Develop Teacher Leaders 69

Chapter 6 • Transforming the School 73

Celebrate Your Success 74

Revising the Process 75

Pacing Guides 76

Revisiting Assessments 76

Data-Based Culture and Climate 78

Chapter 7 • Final Words of Advice 81

Appendix: The Principal's Office 83

References 115

About the Authors

Todd Stanley has been a classroom teacher for the past seventeen years in a myriad of positions. He spent the first five years of his career compacting gifted curriculum in a junior high program called Horizons. The next three years were as a facilitator at the Christopher Program, a project-based, interdisciplinary program involving language arts and social studies for juniors and seniors from around central Ohio. He then created the Ivy Program, a gifted pullout for third and fourth graders. At the same time, he traveled around the state of Ohio for the Literacy Curriculum Alignment Program, training school staffs on how to write common formative assessments and align their curricula. Then he spent four years teaching project-based learning in both social studies and science to fifth and sixth graders at a gifted magnet program called Quest.

He recently had the pleasure of helping create a gifted academy for grades five through eight in the Reynoldsburg (Ohio) Schools called the Gateway Gifted Academy, where educators employ STEM, inquiry-based learning, and project-based learning. He is currently the gifted coordinator for Reynoldsburg Schools and lives in Pickerington, Ohio, with his wife, Nicki, and two daughters, Anna and Abby.

This is his fourth book with Eye On Education. With co-writer Betsy Moore, he wrote the books *Short-Cycle Assessment: Improving Student Achievement through Formative Assessment*, *Critical Thinking and Formative Assessments: Increasing the Rigor in Your Classroom*, and *Formative Assessments in a Professional Learning Community*. He also has written the book *Project-Based Learning for Gifted Students: A Handbook for the 21st Century* for Prufrock Press.

Dr. Jana Alig is a lifelong learner with varied experience in the education arena. Jana has been a special education teacher, a general education teacher, a gifted cluster teacher, an educational consultant, a district special education coordinator, and an elementary school principal; she is currently the director of elementary education for Reynoldsburg City Schools in Reynoldsburg, Ohio.

Jana earned her bachelor of science degree in elementary and special education from Ball State University in Muncie, Indiana. She earned her master's degree in learning disabilities and emotional disorders from Old Dominion University in Norfolk, Virginia, and her Ph.D. in educational leadership and policy with an emphasis in educational administration at Ohio State University.

Throughout her career, Jana has worked with educators to develop principals and teachers as leaders in data analysis, data-based instruction, formative assessments, differentiated instruction, inquiry-based learning, blended learning, and recently in the Common Core State Standards. She has successful experience in transforming schools from low-performing to high-performing organizations, especially with high populations of students at risk. Jana has high expectations for students, teachers, and principals and works diligently to help them reach their goals. Jana lives in Pickerington, Ohio, with her daughter, Hanna, and their dog, Oreo.

Pre-Assessment: Formative Assessment #1

Here is your first assessment. This is a pre-assessment to see how much you already know about formative assessments and using them to create meaningful data that can transform students, teachers, and schools.

1. What is the difference between formative and summative assessments?

2. What advantage does formative assessment have over summative assessment?

3. How can common formative assessments be used to bring about change in a school?

4. Why is it important that common formative assessments be both reliable and valid?

5. How will the SCORE Process provide professional development for a teaching staff?

6. What are the two most important factors when administering common formative assessments?

7. What are effective ways to organize data so it can be put to meaningful use?

8. Once the data is organized, what are ways to analyze it to improve student achievement?

9. Using the information gathered from the common formative assessments, how can the school leader be purposeful in the transformation of the building?

10. How can school leaders ensure that the common formative assessments measure what they want them to?

If you know all the answers to these questions, this book is not for you; you have no need for it. If, however, the questions cause you to be curious about how formative assessments might lead to the transformation of your students, staff, and school, this book will be very helpful.

Using Formative Assessment to Transform Your School

The task of the leader is to get his people from
where they are to where they have not been.
—Henry A. Kissinger

A s a school leader, you have a lot of responsibilities—anything from student discipline to staff morale, from school dances to copy machine mishaps, from snow removal from sidewalks to computer maintenance. Oh, by the way, you are supposed to oversee the learning, nurturing, and well-being of a group of individuals who can sometimes be unwilling to learn new things. Then there are the students to consider. Sometimes this gets overlooked in the hustle and bustle of running the day-to-day operation of a school, that the entire purpose of a school is to provide a place for children to learn and grow to become the best they can be. The question is how much of your very busy day do you actually get to devote to the teaching and learning process?

Being a school leader is a thankless job—a task that, if you do everything correctly, has few if any accolades, little recognition, and rare moments of gratitude. Yet you have chosen to do this important work. In addition, you are reading this book, so you have chosen to make the task even more difficult by seeking to transform your school. You are not satisfied to maintain the status quo but wish to improve both student achievement and teacher growth through professional development. Let us take this opportunity to pat you on the back and say thank you. It might be the only time you experience this during the process, but we want to make sure you know your efforts are appreciated. Education needs more people like you, people willing to take a chance and change business as usual. Change is always very challenging, especially with teachers. As soon as you try something new, a veteran staff member recalls how every few years someone tries something like this without much success. Or you receive calls from parents wondering why you are trying to do things different from when they were in school twenty years before. Even the students, who should be more flexible to change than anyone, grumble when they experience a different routine.

Someone needs to take the lead and envision a better school—one in which students achieve higher results and more importantly learn to be critical problem solvers, one where teachers are able to become better educators, a school the community is proud of and sings its praises rather than begrudges its failure. Who better than you—the school leader, the person who has the single most influence over the school, besides the school secretary (of course) to lead the way?

Using formative assessments as a tool to realize the vision of a higher-achieving school is a wise decision. We have used this formative assessment process all over the state of Ohio and, through our series of books, all over the nation. The one factor all the buildings that experienced significant increases in student achievement and staff development had in common was a supportive leader trumpeting the process. This might have been a principal, a superintendent, a curriculum coordinator, or even a classroom teacher. He or she bought into the process and helped to foster it along the way. This school leader was the cheerleader, teacher, and navigator. On the converse side, the building that experienced little change typically had a school leader who was not on board with the formative assessment process or did not understand the significance of the data and its use. He or she saw it as a mandate from the central office and a means to control what happened in the school.

This book breaks down the common formative assessment process into manageable steps and shows you how to transform your building into a vision of learning for all students. Chapter 1 makes the argument for why schools should use formative assessments in the first place—what the many advantages of using them are and what they will allow your school to achieve. Chapter 2 looks at specific types of formative assessments—what each one is designed to do and how to ensure it is effective. Chapter 3 looks at how your building will develop when it uses common formative assessments to help with instruction. It shows your school how to create its own common formative assessments in order to make classrooms and instruction individualized learning experiences for students and, once the assessments are created, what method ensures the common formative assessments are valid and reliable to provide the needed data. In order for this process to work, the proper tone and environment must be struck at the school. This does not just happen; it must be planned and implemented by design. This is what Chapter 4 helps with. Chapter 5 looks at effective tools for breaking down the data and what the data might mean for a school. Like many things in education, just because school staff members have the data does not mean things will magically begin to change. The data must be disseminated and strategies must be developed on how to improve both student achievement and staff professional development. Finally, once the process is up and running, how will it transform the school into a learning institute where all involved are there to accomplish the same goal? How will you keep this process going so that transformation can continue? This is discussed in Chapter 6.

In order to help you develop common formative assessments in your building, we have created an appendix at the back of the book titled The Principal's Office. Normally, this is a place no one wants to go because it means someone is in trouble. In this case, you want to go to the Principal's Office because it provides resources, reproducibles, and other tools to assist you in your journey.

As the leader, you have the ability to transform your school using the formative assessment process and improve both student learning and teacher pedagogy. For this to happen, you must lead the charge. It will not be easy. There will be times when you feel the process is not working, and you will want to give up. We promise you this: if you stand firm with the formative assessment process, if you lead by example and show your students and staff that you buy into the process, they will be more motivated to buy into it themselves. School leaders, like teachers, sometimes forget the influence they have—that by leading by example, people are much more willing to follow than if someone is just barking orders.

By reading this book, you have already begun to lead by example. Many times the most difficult task in a long journey is taking the first step in the right direction. This book will help you, the teachers, and the students learn and experience that it is not just about reaching the destination; it is the journey that is the most beneficial.

chapter one

Why Use Formative Assessments?

When the cook tastes the soup, that's formative assessment; when the customer tastes the soup, that's summative assessment (Paul Black, 1998).

Rethinking Assessments

School reform in the United States has been going on for hundreds of years. Since the time the first school opened in the United States, people have been trying to improve schools by doing such things as switching the desk from the back of the seat to the front or moving from slate chalkboards to interactive whiteboards. Many of these changes have to do with technology—from the mechanical pencils that have replaced the quill and ink to the software teachers use to conduct interviews with people half a world away. At the same time, how much has school pedagogy guided by assessment really changed over the past two hundred years? How difficult would it be for a time traveler from the 1800s to walk into a classroom, see the teacher at the front of the room reciting a lesson while the students sit and listen, and not figure out what setting they are in? Teachers follow the same basic formula their predecessors did hundreds of years ago: present a lesson, then test students at the end of the lesson on what they were supposed to learn before moving on to the next bit of material and repeating the process. The assessment is used primarily to give students an evaluation of how much of the material they learned, but where are the assurances that the students have mastered the concepts? How does this summative assessment process prevent students who did not learn the material from falling through the cracks? Educators need a barometer of where students are at any given time. That is where formative assessments come into play.

Formative assessments evaluate where the students have been, where they are now, and where they are going. The formative assessment process is different from the teach-test method; it is more like the assess-plan-teach cyclical process. It is certainly a different way to run the instructional process in your school.

Think of a formative assessment like a doctor treating a patient. A doctor typically does three things when trying to help a patient. The first thing is to take a history of the patient: Is there a past history of this illness? Did the patient have similar symptoms at an earlier time? How long have the symptoms been going on? Second, the doctor assesses the current symptoms: listens to the breathing, checks vitals, runs tests. Third, the doctor treats the symptoms with therapy, medicine, whatever it takes. Throughout the process, the doctor gives small formative assessments to determine the best course of treatment. After the patient is feeling better, the doctor conducts a summative test that is designed to make sure the treatment was successful. Education puts the emphasis on this follow-up. Educators are not checking the history, not treating the symptoms—just conducting the follow-up. What happens if by this time, the student is already disengaged because of boredom or overwhelmed by the time taking assessments? Educators need to make sure students are getting the proper treatment just as patients expect their doctors to do. Teachers need to do the history, to see what students know and do not know. How can a teacher determine what to teach without knowing what knowledge students already possess? Teachers must monitor students' progress of understanding, especially deficits, before assessing them at the end to see if teaching was successful. No teacher wants to lose a student who does not understand a concept; that student should be nursed along the way to ensure a successful prognosis into the future.

Formative assessments allow teachers to do just that. By performing a pretest, a teacher can see what students know, pinpointing what needs to be taught and in how much depth. A formative assessment along the way shows whether students are understanding and learning. If they are not, the teacher needs to slow down or approach the concept from another perspective to help students understand. If students are mastering the concept, the teacher needs to decide whether to spend more time teaching it, put the time toward some other concept, or go deeper with a topic in project-based learning. By the time the summative assessment comes, the teacher has taken the students' history and monitored understanding along the way, using the formative assessment data and individualized instruction so that students are successful.

The Pudding

Enough telling about the effects of common formative assessments. We want to show just how effective they can be by using exactly what we preach in this book: data. The Coalition of Essential Schools went into numerous schools in Ohio, bringing a process of formative assessment called LCAP (Literacy Curriculum Alignment Program). Figure 1.1 (pages 8–9) shows the gains using the formative assessment process in these schools in a study by Dr. Susan Lang as part of her doctoral dissertation.

As you can see from the data, most districts improved their scores. Some districts that had been at risk and on academic watch, such as Nelsonville, saw significant increases once the process was used, transforming them to the effective designation. Another example of formative assessment success is at French Run Elementary in Reynoldsburg City Schools. Teachers there used a combination of common quarterly formative assessments as well as what they termed weekly exit cards. Students received exit cards at the end of each week to check for understanding of concepts being taught. The data was collected weekly and analyzed by teachers and the principal to determine growth. When growth was not being detected, they put in place interventions such as mini-lessons, individualized tutoring, and whole-group review. When growth was shown, teachers moved into deeper concepts, expanding students' knowledge. Using these strategies, the school went from the district's lowest performing elementary school based on state assessment in the 2005–2006 school year, to being designated by the state as a School of Promise as well as earning the ranking of Excellent with Distinction in the 2007–2008 school year. This transformation took place in just two years.

· Figure 1.1a Quantitative Findings of Cumulative Gains in Reading Proficiency

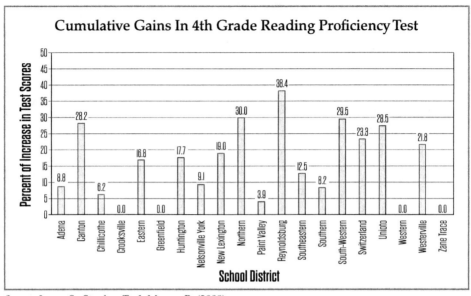

Source: Lang, S., Stanley, T., & Moore, B. (2008)

· Figure 1.1b Quantitative Findings of Cumulative Gains in Math Proficiency

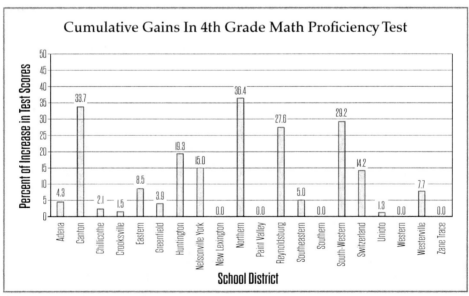

Source: Lang, S., Stanley, T., & Moore, B. (2008)

• **Figure 1.1c** Quantitative Findings (*continued*)

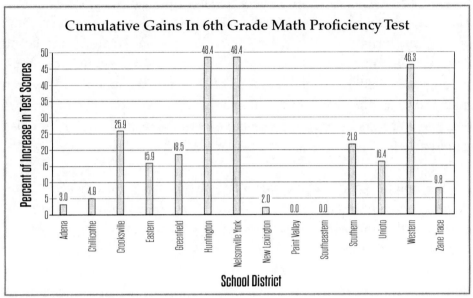

Source: Lang, S., Stanley, T., & Moore, B. (2008)

• **Figure 1.1d** Quantitative Findings (*continued*)

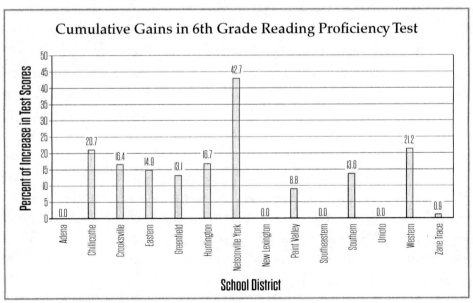

Source: Lang, S., Stanley, T., & Moore, B. (2008)

In addition to these studies, national studies have shown the effectiveness of formative assessments in regard to improving student achievement. The groundbreaking study in 1998 by Black and Young made some compelling conclusions about assessment, including that "there is significant evidence that improving formative assessment improves student learning" (Young & Giebelhaus, 2005). Because of this conclusion, one suggestion they gave was that "more frequent shorter tests are preferable to less frequent longer tests"—a call for formative assessments, which are administered periodically; a summative assessment is given only at the end of a course of study.

The Silicon Valley Mathematics Initiative, through the Noyce Foundation, conducted a study both of schools using formative assessments and those that did not. The study found significant improvements in the number of students who met the standards involved in using formative assessments compared with those who did not use the process (Foster & Poppers, 2009). Similarly, Lisa W. Smith in her doctoral thesis studied the effects of formative assessment on 2,900 sixth, seventh, and eighth graders in north Georgia and found there was much improvement in test results for those schools that used the process (Smith, 2008).

Formative assessments can be used not only to improve the achievement of students but also to predict how the students might perform on the mastery of certain standards. In March of 2009, the Massachusetts Department of Secondary Education released a report showing that formative assessments indicated eighty-three percent to ninety-one percent accuracy when forecasting the mastery of mathematics standards. Educators could use results from formative assessments to help predict results on high-stakes testing, giving them a better idea of student achievement and where intervention might be needed—the doctor looking for symptoms that might lead to larger problems. Something can be done about symptoms found early; the longer one waits, the more difficult they may be to treat. The Massachusetts report also showed that schools that used formative assessments over the period from 2001 to 2007 outperformed similar schools that did not use formative assessments. With results such as these, what educator would not want to use formative assessment to help with student achievement and drive instruction?

The Advantages of Formative Assessments

Specifically, what are the advantages of formative assessments? The most obvious one is that students get a better education. Numerous studies have shown that not all students learn the same way. Yet many traditional classrooms are set up to teach to one type of student. With the summative assessment process, the teacher leads the entire class toward one test. The formative assessment process allows the teacher to tailor the learning to specific students. This way, students receive a specialized education that allows them to build on strengths and improve weaknesses. One of the big concerns about educational institutions is that because they are so large, teachers end up teaching to the middle and hoping students at the low end catch up, while students at the other end get enough knowledge to satisfy them. With formative assessments, students at each level get what they need to grow as learners.

Here are some of the advantages of formative assessments broken down:

■ **Check of Understanding:** The entire purpose of the formative assessment process is to see what students know and are able to understand. Thus, a successful formative assessment checks for student understanding. How nice it would be as a teacher to have an icon above each student's head indicating how much of the lesson he or she understands. Unfortunately, we do not have these, so teachers use informal cues: Does the student seem to be paying attention? making eye contact? raising a hand or shaking the head when asked about understanding? But how reliable are these cues? Could a student look right at the teacher and not have a clue what the teacher is talking about? How many students who seem not to be paying attention at all can shoot off a correct answer when called on? Formative assessments are a more reliable and objective way to check for understanding. They need not be huge productions with pencils, optical answer sheets, or booklets. Asking a student a question to check for understanding, sitting down one-on-one with a student and having a conversation about the student's level of understanding, or presenting a quick, weekly, two- to three-question quiz—any of these provides reliable feedback on whether your students understand the material.

- Teaching Assessment: This benefit will probably be very important to you as a school leader. Formative assessment results can reveal strengths and weaknesses of teaching skills. Does an instructor teach certain subjects really well? Is the teacher talented at breaking down certain concepts for students? Does the teacher need some professional development around certain skills? We will talk more in depth about this in Chapter 5, but how you use this information is going to make or break the formative assessment process with your teaching staff. If you use it against them as an evaluation, teachers may become mistrustful of the assessment process and be hesitant to use it. However, if it is used to strengthen teacher skills and is backed with good professional development, the teachers will see it as an opportunity to become better at the profession they so dearly love. There will be some tough conversations about the data that comes out of the assessments, and some teachers will think you are out to get them, but in reality, all educators want what is best for kids, and sometimes that means a change in teaching and learning. As noted before, schools have not advanced much when it comes to pedagogy. What would happen to a telephone company or a computer company that did not adjust to the times? Schools should not be left behind with VCRs and eight-track players. Companies today call for their newest employees to have twenty-first-century skills. In order to offer those, students need twenty-first-century schools. That means transforming the way students are taught.

- Flexibility: Summative assessments are typically given at one time and one time only: at the end of the instruction. Formative assessments can be given whenever the teacher needs to get a gauge on student learning. For instance, science teacher Mr. Brooks begins a unit on the solar system. He conducts the first activity, and students' hands are shooting up like fireworks. Before he can even finish a question, students are raising their hands to answer it. It seems very obvious that this class has a lot of prior knowledge regarding the solar system. The only question is, how much? Mr. Brooks decides to give the final assessment during the very next class. He will not use the results as grades, though; he uses the assessment as a diagnostic tool to gather information about what the students know. If the students can all pass the test, then what would be the point in going forward with the unit as it is? Mr. Brooks has two options: (1) give students credit for the unit based on the results of the formative assessment and move on to something new, or (2) develop another unit on the solar system that goes more in-depth and challenges students at a higher level of thinking. Either way, the students are learning at their level rather than the level of the curriculum.

A formative assessment does not have to be given just at the beginning of a unit either. At any time, a teacher may determine that monitoring student learning would be beneficial. Another example is a teacher gets halfway through a unit on negative numbers. Homework is coming back showing that students just are not getting the concept as quickly as the teacher thought. This homework can be used as the formative assessment to determine that the concept either needs to be retaught or needs to be broken down further to ensure that students get an understanding of the concept of negative numbers.

■ **Easy Implementation:** Formative assessments are easy to implement. As seen in the two examples just given, a formative assessment need not be a formal assessment or even a pencil-to-paper activity. In the first example, the teacher observed that the students knew the material. In the second example, the teacher used homework that was already being given to determine that they were not demonstrating understanding. Although this book will show you how to create your own, common assessments that will get the data needed for student and staff improvement, formative assessments need not be of this type to be effective. Once teachers get used to the idea of using formative assessments, they will realize they have been using them for years in sporadic fashion; they just did not call them formative assessments or intentionally use the data to guide instruction. And the more comfortable teachers become with the process, the more comfortable they will be creating their own informal formative assessments to use with students to help inform instruction.

■ **Curriculum Guidance:** The most effective use of formative assessments is to provide an individualized, personal learning experience for students. The learning is going to stand a better chance of being more meaningful for students because it is tailored to their needs.

A student need not be bored being retaught something already learned. The formative assessment has shown the student already knows it, and something else more meaningful can be taught in its place. Another student in the same class does not need to worry about being left behind, because the use of formative assessments lets the teacher know the foundation skills for learning need to be broken down and to provide additional remediation.

You have probably heard the saying "the cart pushing the horse." Assessments are the horse that should be driving curriculum in education. By focusing on summative assessments, educators wait until the end to see if students actually learned the curriculum and thus let the cart push the horse. Formative assessments allow teachers to shape curriculum based upon the results of the formative assessment. In essence, formative assessments are the horses pulling the carts or the curriculum—the way it was meant to be.

Answer to Formative Assessment Question #1: What is the difference between formative and summative assessments?

The difference between a formative assessment and a summative assessment is found in the names. A summative assessment is the *sum* of the work that has already been taught. It determines how much the students learned. A formative assessment *forms* the instruction. It determines how much the student already knows as well as how much the student still needs to learn. From the formative assessment, a teacher can clearly plan a lesson that meets the needs of the student.

Answer to Formative Assessment Question #2: What advantage does formative assessment have over summative assessment?

The most important advantage to using a formative assessment over a summative assessment is a teacher does not have to guess how a student is going to perform. Formative assessments can predict what students can achieve. Because of this, formative assessments drive instruction and result in higher student achievement and better teaching—both goals you want for your building as its school leader.

chapter two

How You Can Use Formative Assessment

Formative assessment is about assessment for learning
as opposed to summative where assessment is of learning
(DuFour, DuFour, Eaker, & Many, 2010).

What Is a Formative Assessment?

It is important to determine a clear definition for formative assessment. According to Learn NC of the University of North Carolina website, formative assessments are

> … ongoing observations and methods of evaluation designed to measure student comprehension of a concept or task in order to identify areas that require enhanced or adapted instruction. It emphasizes the mastery of classroom content instead of the earning of grades or test scores and is conducted throughout the entire instructional process to gauge students' progress. Results are then used to adapt instruction to meet students' needs. Feedback is also used to help students achieve their learning goals and takes the form of specific suggestions for improvement and discussion of errors rather than merely providing the correct answer. (LEARNNC, University of North Carolina).

The most important aspect of this definition is that formative assessment *informs instruction*. In other words, teachers use information gathered from the formative assessment to determine not only what will be taught but also at what depth. As the quote at the beginning of this chapter stated; teachers are assessing for learning rather than assessing of learning. Additionally, the idea of emphasizing the mastery of classroom content rather than the earning of grades is essential. This is a check to see where students are and where they need to go. Teachers are forming the lesson from the students' knowledge and understanding.

W. James Popham in his book *Transformative Assessment* offers an even simpler definition: "Formative assessment is a planned process in which teachers or students use assessment-based evidence to adjust what they're currently doing" (Popham, 2008).

What do you as the school leader get from the formative assessment process? You get evidence that students are growing a year's worth of development in a year's time. Formative assessment data used effectively pushes students and provides students additional foundation in skills they may be lacking. What educators would not want this for their students? But this pedagogy process is much easier to agree to in theory than in practice. Such a concept requires that teachers have fluid lesson plans that are massaged and adapted on a daily basis for individual students. Differentiation must occur in the classroom so that students are taught differently according to their needs. This certainly seems to make more work for the teacher. It might involve more lesson plans, alternative lessons and assessments, flexible grouping, and other such strategies. Teachers who like to teach the same lesson plans over and over every year without any adaptation of those lessons to the needs of the students will be challenged. Again we come back to this: what is best for kids?

What Are Common Formative Assessments?

When looking at the entire school, how can student achievement be improved? In comparing one classroom of students with another, what common factor indicates that all students are demonstrating understanding? Common formative assessments provide this common factor for comparing and identifying strengths among teachers and growth of students in the same subject or grade level. When all teachers of similar subject areas or grade levels give the same assessment, they can compare apples to apples rather than apples to oranges. Otherwise, if two teachers use different assessments to evaluate their students, one assessment might be quite challenging, while the other asks lower level questions that are not a challenge. A high score in one of the classes might not match up with the skills learned in the other class. Having a common assessment means evaluating students using the same criteria. How can a teacher be sure the common assessment is truly indicating mastery of the Common Core State Standards (CCSS), though?

Teachers can start with the defining characteristics of common formative assessment. According to Larry Ainsworth and Donald Viegut in their book *Common Formative Assessments: How to Connect Standard-Based Instruction and Assessment* (2006), common formative assessments are defined under the following criteria:

- Periodic or interim assessments should be collaboratively designed by grade-level or course teams of teachers

- Assessments should be designed as pre- and post-assessments to ensure same-assessment comparison of student growth

- Assessments must be similar in design and format to district and state assessments

- Items on the assessments should represent essential standards only

- Assessments must include a blend of item types, including multiple choice and constructed response (short or extended)

- Assessments must be administered to all students in grade level or course several times during the quarter, semester, trimester, or entire school year

- Student results should be analyzed in data teams to guide instructional planning and delivery

The rest of this book is devoted to taking you through these steps, helping you as a school leader to create common formative assessments with your team, and explaining how to use the information gleaned from them to improve student achievement and staff professional development.

What Are the Advantages of Common Formative Assessments?

The *Princeton Review* (Marshall, 2005) mentions the benefits of formative assessment at several levels:

- In the classroom, students better understand their own strengths and weaknesses and can chart a course to mastery.

- Teachers can monitor the effectiveness of their instruction and adjust their work based on solid student achievement data.

- Administrators can use formative assessment at the district level to monitor individual school performance and provide assistance and intervention as necessary.

The benefit of common formative assessment is that it works at all levels. Students, teachers, and administrators get information that assists them in helping students learn and grow.

For students, formative assessments show strengths and acknowledge success while at the same time showing where improvement can be made. Knowing ones' strengths and weaknesses can be very valuable. Teachers are responsible for looking at the data to figure out how best to work with each student. Then the teachers and students can work on improving the weaknesses and bolstering the strengths.

Teachers can also discern their own strengths and weaknesses. If a math teacher gets consistent data that students do not understand geometry concepts, maybe that is a subject the teacher is not comfortable with; the teacher may want to seek additional professional development. The formative assessment process also allows teachers to do something they do not get the opportunity to do very often: collaborate with purpose. Take the math teacher whose students are struggling with geometry. If another teacher is identified as being quite strong with the geometry standards, these two can be paired and collaborate, strengthening the skills of the teacher who is not getting the desired results. For such pairing to be successful, the school leader needs to provide common time for teachers to go over the data as a team to figure out patterns and work together. We will talk about how this can work in a later chapter.

Finally, the school leader can use common formative assessments to see where the building is as a whole. Does a group of students need further study in order to understand and master the standards? If so, what are you going to provide as the school leader to make sure that happens? Will you allocate classroom resources? In other words, maybe you need five sections of biology instead of four. Will you provide materials and resources to give students the additional support they need? What workbooks or computer programs can be purchased to offer support? Can you rearrange the schedule to provide additional time? One of the high schools we worked with had flexible, grouped study halls that changed every month. Using the formative assessments, teachers placed each student in the study hall with the teacher who could provide the additional instruction the assessment indicated the student needed. So struggling readers would be assigned to a study hall with the language arts teacher who offered support and instruction to catch the students up. Then after a month, the students took another formative assessment to determine whether they had improved or needed to stay in the language arts study hall for more instruction. Students who improved might be moved to another study hall for support in another area or assigned to a general study hall if no additional support was deemed necessary. Are you going to provide tutoring after school? This calls for a district willing to offer the funds and staff members willing to offer their time. There are several possibilities for impacting student learning once you have identified a need.

The school leader also has a large impact on the professional development of the teaching staff. If a teacher is struggling with certain standards, the school leader has to be an instructional leader and provide needed professional development. The school leader needs to plan and be creative in carving out time for collaboration and additional professional development opportunities to meet the needs of the teachers, just as a teacher would do for students. Does the school have a mentoring program in which teachers with a track record of success can work with teachers who need support in identified areas?

We like to boil down the advantages of common formative assessments into what we term the four Es.

> **Exposure:** To give students planned and purposeful *exposure* to the standards and assessment formats

Expertise: To develop *expertise* in each teacher's ability to ask higher-level questions, base instructional decisions for delivery on performance data, and collaborate for curricular direction across grade levels

Endurance: To build persistence and *endurance* for each student to be able to (1) build lasting stamina through the long test and (2) work through difficult questions

Empower: To *empower* teachers, students, and parents to become responsible decision makers for learning

We will go into further detail concerning the four Es in Chapter 4, but know that by using the common formative assessment, you are ultimately doing what is best for kids.

When Do You Use Formative Assessments?

Because formative assessments can be given at almost any time, when is a good time to give common formative assessments? It is important to grease the skids, so to speak, with students regarding formative assessments. What we mean by this is if the only formative assessments students receive are the common school-wide ones, their experience with them is not going to be as effective as could be. Thus, you should encourage your colleagues to use formative assessments on a weekly if not daily basis. An assessment can be something as simple as a question of the week, in which students are asked a weekly pre- and post-test question to see what they understood and if they now understand it better. Or the assessment could be a warm-up question dealing with the lesson of that day to see how many students already have knowledge about the topic.

Formative assessments need not be formal for everyday classroom use. Listed here from the West Virginia Department of Education are a variety of formative assessments. There is a brief explanation of each located in the Principal's Office of this book (page 84).

Observations	Questioning
Discussion	Exit Slips/Admit Slips
Learning Logs/Response Logs	Graphic Organizers
Peer/Self-Assessments	Practice Presentations

Visual Representations	Kinesthetic Assessments
Individual Whiteboards	Laundry Day
Four Corners	Constructive Quizzes
Think-Pair-Share	Appointment Clock
As I See It	

Some of these examples, such as the individual whiteboards and the constructive quizzes, are quite easy. They also give you immediate feedback on whether instruction needs to be adapted or not. For instance, attaching a student response to the whiteboard provides a quick, easy way to administer, grade, and discuss content with students. Others, such as questioning (in which teachers must ask better questions to check for understanding) and discussion, might require some teacher training. That can be as easy as identifying teachers who are good at either and having them lead an informal workshop during a staff meeting or Professional Learning Community time on how to improve these assessment methods in the classroom. Kinesthetic assessments, think-pair-share, and four corners are effective because they get students out of their seats and allow them to share their understanding with others. Teachers can document and record who is demonstrating understanding and who needs more practice.

No matter which formative assessment a teacher uses for his or her classroom, it provides feedback for that group of students. Depending on the variety of students in a class, the teacher might even choose various formative assessments for the same activity. Some students might not have the maturity to handle the self/peer-assessments, other students might need the assessment broken down further and can use graphic organizers to do so, and others might be ready for a kinesthetic assessment.

Using formative assessments regularly in your classroom has advantages. Wiliam and Thompson (2007) point out several:

- Clarifying and sharing learning intentions and criteria for success

- Engineering effective classroom discussions, questions, and learning tasks that elicit evidence of learning

- Providing feedback that moves learners forward

- Activating students as instructional resources for one another

- Activating students as the owners of their own learning

Each teacher can decide what form of formative assessment to use, but having it as a common part of class will pave the way for better results. When school-wide common formative assessments are given and data is collected, students will be familiar with them and how to use the data to set their own goals for learning.

At the very least, you should conduct common formative assessments each quarter. When we worked with schools in Ohio, we recommended one at the end of each grading quarter. This was used as a diagnostic assessment. In other words, it was not used as a summative assessment in order to determine a grade in the class. Instead it was used to see which standards students understood well and which ones still needed more work. In analyzing the data in teams, as Ainsworth and Viegut suggest, we determined what needed to be covered in more depth or what needed review. Teachers could then adjust their instruction to meet these needs, often collaborating to do so.

Ideally, administering formative assessments more often than once a quarter provides a better understanding of student learning. Exit cards are an option for using common formative assessments in a daily or weekly format. Exit cards are designed around a specific learning target. Students have to complete the task before exiting the school at the end of the class, day, or week. These may be teacher constructed during grade-level or department meetings. These tasks may be performance, constructed-response, or multiple-choice format. The exit cards should take ten to fifteen minutes to administer to students. These provide a quick, effective way of collecting meaningful data on students and their learning.

The school leader then uses the data from the exit cards to engage in meaningful discussions with teachers about why their students are successful or what might need to be done to help students. The school leader can also have conversations with students. A student who is close to high achievement and just needs a push in the right direction might be inspired by a kind word or note from the school leader. Similarly, the data might be used to bring about dialogue with parents about their children and what could be done at home to foster student skills.

Answer to Formative Assessment Question #3: How can common formative assessments be used to bring about change in a school?

How formative assessments can be used to bring about change varies. Teachers can use daily or weekly formative assessments to get an idea of how best to proceed with instruction. Common formative assessments that are given to students at regular intervals allow a school leader to discern information about how the students and building are doing regarding the identified important CCSS. Curriculum, materials, resources, and staff can be adjusted to improve student achievement as shown by the common formative assessment. This will provoke a change, resulting in higher student achievement and a stronger teaching staff.

chapter three

Developing Valid and Reliable Assessments

*A school must use assessments that actually
measure the content that teachers teach* (Marzano, 2003).

Two important aspects to consider when developing assessments are
reliability and *validity.* It is important to define these terms.

> Reliability is defined as the extent to which a questionnaire, test,
> observation or any measurement procedure produces the same
> results on repeated trials. In short, it is the stability or consistency
> of scores over time or across raters. Keep in mind that reliability
> pertains to scores not people. Thus, in research we would never
> say that someone was reliable. As an example, consider judges in
> a platform diving competition. The extent to which they agree on
> the scores for each contestant is an indication of reliability. Sim-
> ilarly, the degree to which an individual's responses (i.e., their
> scores) on a survey would stay the same over time is also a sign
> of reliability. An important point to understand is that a measure
> can be perfectly reliable and yet not be valid. (Miller, 2011)

When an assessment is reliable, it gives you replicable results.

⸬ Figure 3.1 Three Types of Validity

Type of Validity	Definition	Example/Non-Example
Content	The extent to which the content of the test matches the instructional objectives	A semester or quarterly exam that includes only content covered during the past six weeks is not a valid measure of the course's overall objectives—it has very low content validity.
Criterion	The extent to which scores on the test are in agreement with (concurrent validity) or predict (predictive validity) an external criterion	If the fourth-grade end-of-year math tests correlate highly with the statewide math tests, they have high concurrent validity.
Construct	The extent to which an assessment corresponds to other variables, as predicted by some rationale or theory	If you can correctly hypothesize that English language learners will perform differently on a reading test than English-speaking students (because of theory), the assessment may have construct validity.

Source: Florida Center for Instructional Technology, 2012

Validity, on the other hand, is whether an assessment really measures what it is intended to measure. For an assessment to be valid, it must demonstrate reliable results. Validity can be measured in three ways, as shown in Figure 3.1. In order to have confidence that a test is valid (and therefore that the inferences made based on the test scores are valid), all three kinds of validity evidence should be considered.

When creating assessments, reliability and validity are essential. Without these components, assessments are worthless. This may seem like common sense, but an assessment audit in any school will reveal many assessments that are either not reliable or invalid.

Let us look at a sixth-grade CCSS reading standard for literature:

> Explain how an author develops the point of view of the narrator or speaker in a text.

The following multiple-choice question was given to sixth graders to measure this standard.

What is the point of view in a text?

    a. the setting of the story

    b. the perspective the story is told from

    c. the action the story hinges on

    d. a prediction the story makes

The multiple-choice question contains terms from the standard: *point of view* and *text*. Students who answered this question correctly demonstrated knowing the definition of *point of view*. This question may be reliable, but it is not valid. In assessing the standard, the question should measure whether students are able to explain how an author develops the point of view of the narrator or speaker in a text. A more aligned question might be this:

Which of the following is a method an author would use to develop point of view in a text?

    a. using dialogue to reveal a character's thoughts

    b. choosing a setting that directly affects the story

    c. choosing an antagonist who is sympathetic to the audience

    d. choosing a narrator who is interesting to the audience

This question has strong content validity. The student has to look at the different choices and determine a strategy the author could use to develop point of view. Another way of assessing this standard is to have students complete a constructed-response question to a particular text. For example, the following:

How does the author develop the point of view of Katniss in Chapter 5 of the *Hunger Games*? Provide two examples from the text to illustrate the author's strategy.

Having the student indicate examples and the strategy used within the given text provides a strong content-valid and reliable question for this standard statement.

The most important aspect of writing formative assessments, or any assessment for that matter, is to make sure the questions show consistent results (reliability) and that the skill and level of understanding the standard requires the student to demonstrate is addressed by the question or even a series of questions (validity).

That is why when your school goes to write its common formative assessments, using a process that allows for valid and reliable assessments is important. Such a process is the SCORE Process.

The SCORE Process

As a school leader, a simple process you can teach your staff to use when developing common formative assessments is one called the SCORE Process. This was outlined at length in the book *Short-Cycle Assessment: Improving Student Achievement Through Formative Assessment* (Lang, Stanley, & Moore, 2008), but we will explain the basics of it here. SCORE stands for the following:

S Short

C Cycle Assessments

O Organized for

R Results and

E Expectations

SCORE is a process that takes teachers step-by-step through the creation of formative assessments. The SCORE Process involves seven steps:

1. Understanding the Common Core State Standards and state assessments
2. Developing a pacing guide
3. Designing an assessment
4. Administering the assessment
5. Analyzing the data from the assessment
6. Making instructional improvements based on the data
7. Revising the Process

Rather than viewing the process as a list of items that need to be checked off, we like to think of the process as cyclical and looking more like Figure 3.2.

· **Figure 3.2** The First Three Steps of the SCORE Process

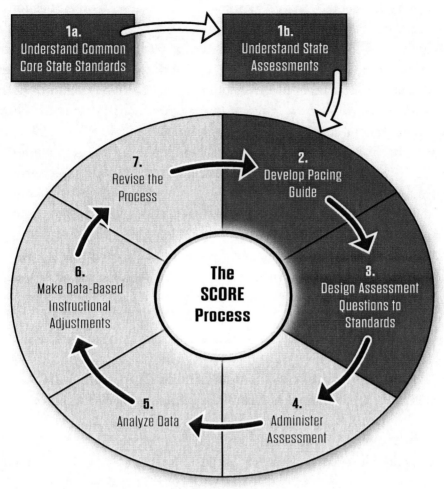

This chapter takes you through the first three steps of the SCORE Process, which are designed to make sure assessments are both valid and reliable.

Step One: Understanding the Common Core State Standards (CCSS) and State Assessments

Prior to developing any kind of common formative assessment, it is important to first understand what students need to learn. In this day of standards-based learning, most subject areas and grade levels are tied to academic content standards developed at either the state or the national level, as in the case of the CCSS. The standards are the valid foundation for the state assessments.

One rationale for creating common formative assessments is that through the development of the questions and pacing guide, teachers learn exactly what the standards mean and at what thinking level the standards need to be taught, making the staff better able to teach the standards to the students. Numerous times in our trainings, productive discussions have broken out among faculty as to the interpretation of a CCSS. For instance, what *formal style* in language arts means exactly. Or who is to blame for the failure of Reconstruction after the Civil War. It is always interesting to watch as people who have different perspectives explain their understanding of the same CCSS. Teachers learn from one another and grow as educators through such discussions.

The collaborative process of developing the common formative assessment is in itself valuable professional development for a teaching staff. It requires teachers to think collaboratively about what students have to know and do to show they understand the CCSS. The role of the school leader is to foster this type of collaboration. Once they have a better understanding, teachers can use this knowledge in developing lessons and units to guide students to understanding as well.

It is also important to have a familiarity with the assessments your state administers to students. Although each assessment is unique, there are certain commonalities among the types of questions used on standardized assessments. The following types of questions are used: multiple choice, constructed response, response grid, performance tasks, and writing prompts.

Understanding the design of the state standardized assessments guides the format of your own common formative assessment. Most state assessments have published testing blueprints. Check with your state's department of education, or for Common Core State Assessments blueprints, go to the Smarter Balance or PARRC websites, depending on which consortium your state belongs to.

Questions to guide your school's formative assessment design may include the following:

- What types of questions are used on the state assessment?
    - ☐ Multiple choice? If so, how many choices are given?
    - ☐ Constructed response? If so, how much detail is required in the answers?

☐ Response grid? If so, do we use them every day? Do students know how to record answers?

☐ Performance tasks? If so, what rubrics are used?

■ What are the point values of each type of question?

☐ How does the student earn each point available?

■ What is the thinking level indicated in each standard statement to be assessed?

☐ Is the assessment question written to the same level or higher than indicated in the standard statement?

These guiding questions provide a framework for understanding the construct of state assessments and will be used again in revising the common assessments the teaching staff creates. This consistent process helps ensure reliable and valid assessments. Now that the teachers have a good understanding of the CCSS and assessment format, it is time to put everything together into a pacing guide.

Step Two: Developing a Pacing Guide

Developing a pacing guide is the second step in the SCORE Process. A pacing guide is simply a sorting tool used to plan when to assess a particular CCSS during the school year. The pacing guide is divided into columns according to the frequency of assessment during the school year. Most schools have at least one common assessment per grading period. If the grading periods are every nine weeks, there should be four columns on the pacing chart. If grading periods are every six weeks, you might have assessments more frequently. A blank pacing guide is provided in the Principal's Office (page 90).

When developing common formative assessments, teachers need a tool to schedule when particular standards need to be assessed. This assessment pacing guide should align to any curriculum mapping that has already been done at the school, or it may be the foundation of the curriculum mapping that will occur after assessments are created.

When developing a pacing guide, there are several important factors to consider.

■ Although you might teach a skill all the time, you may assess the skill only a handful of times. *The pacing guide is about when you assess.*

- Think about when you want the *information* on whether or not the student has mastered the skill or what progress the student has made toward mastery.

- Think about when you would become *concerned* if the student could not do the skill described in the standard. You should place the standard on the pacing guide before this happens.

- Think about when you would provide *intervention* with regard to the standard.

- If the standard has several skills involved, you may *break* the standard into pieces.

- You may put the standard in *more than one* grading period.

A sample pacing guide for fifth-grade social studies is shown in Figure 3.3. As you can see, it is a simple matter of deciding which standards to assess in which time segment you have decided upon for your formative assessment.

The simplest way to get started on your pacing guide is to assemble all the teachers who teach a grade level and/or subject area to collaboratively agree where they wish to place each standard throughout the school year. Some standards naturally build on one another or chronologically make sense in a particular order. For instance, in math, area cannot be taught until the concept of perimeter has been covered. A social studies teacher would not want to begin with the Civil War and then go back chronologically to the American Revolution. Students will think slavery was abolished before the United States became an independent nation. The expertise and experience of the teaching staff is necessary to determine where to place other standards. The science department might find teaching simpler topics, such as space, makes sense before tackling more complex topics, such as electricity.

If it is difficult to release the entire staff in a given grade level to discuss and debate placement of standards, having representatives from multiple grades is an alternative. These experts set the pacing guide for the school in multiple grade levels, and your responsibility is to communicate the information to the rest of the school.

Another method is to have multiple subject areas collaborate. In the social studies pacing guide sample shown in Figure 3.3, the math teacher might teach the circle graph, or the language arts teacher might gather information from multiple sources. This method allows for collaboration

▪ Figure 3.3 Sample Pacing Guide for Fifth-Grade Social Studies

Grading Period 1	Grading Period 2	Grading Period 3	Grading Period 4
◆ Multiple-tier timelines ◆ Globes and other geographic tools used to make maps ◆ Individuals can better understand public issues by gathering and interpreting information from multiple sources. ◆ Information displayed in circle graphs ◆ The choices people make have both present and future consequences.	◆ Latitude and longitude can be used to make generalizations about climate. ◆ Regions can be determined using various criteria ◆ Variations among physical environments within the Western Hemisphere influence human activities. ◆ Political, environmental, social, and economic factors cause people, products, and ideas to move from place to place.	◆ Early Indian civilizations (Maya, Inca, Aztec, Mississippian) ◆ American Indians developed unique cultures with many different ways of life. ◆ European exploration and colonization ◆ Democracies, dictatorships, and monarchies	◆ Workers can improve their ability to earn income by gaining new knowledge, skills, and experiences. Productive resources promote specialization that leads to trade. ◆ Regions and countries become interdependent when they specialize. ◆ The Western Hemisphere is culturally diverse because of American Indian, European, Asian, and African influences.

among teachers who might not normally get a chance to talk, providing an infusion of new ideas. It also lends itself to cross-curricular lessons and activities, especially if your school uses inquiry-based units or STEM methodology. A math teacher might work with a social studies teacher on the economics standards. They can create a lesson plan together and execute it in both classes so that students experience the CCSS in multiple classes, leading to more real-world connections being made by the students.

Yet another way is to have teacher leaders develop the pacing charts and work in a train-the-trainer model to bring them back to staff. Using this model enhances the interdisciplinary approach to teaching and integrating the standards across disciplines. Whichever method you decide to use, the creation of the pacing guide sets the tone for the rest of the steps in the SCORE Process and guides the creation of questions on the common assessments.

Step Three: Designing an Assessment

The next step is bringing the CCSS to a classroom instruction level. Developing and selecting questions for a common assessment is somewhat tedious work, but it is also when the most "aha moments" for teachers occur. Developing an assessment may be done by writing the questions or by selecting questions that already exist. We strongly recommend writing the questions. "Why should we reinvent the wheel? Isn't there a place we can go online to get questions that address the standard?" teachers often asked us when we told them they should write the questions for their formative assessments. The analogy we like to use with teachers is that of their own students. A student could very well copy the answer to a question; the student gets the correct answer after all. A teacher is usually quick to point out that the student does not learn in this situation. We say the same thing to the teaching staff. By getting the questions from somewhere else, the teachers are missing out on the learning opportunity writing the questions themselves provides. We also often hear this: "I am not a test writer." Our response to that comment usually is, "If you aren't a test writer or an assessment expert, who is?" All teachers need to know how to assess their students formally and informally. Some teachers will need to have professional development around assessment design and how to make sure the assessments they are using in their classrooms are reliable and valid compared to the learning goals set. Part of your role as school leader is identifying these individuals and providing the necessary professional development. This might come in the form of partnering mentor teachers with them, leading a book talk that covers the topic, bringing in outside trainers, or providing the means to attend a workshop that would be beneficial.

Rick DuFour describes an obvious benefit for teachers who create their own formative assessments:

> The best way to do this [develop mastery of standards] is to have teachers … work together to develop assessment techniques, reflect upon their practice, analyze data on student achievement, and generate new strategies for becoming more effective in achieving their shared goals (DuFour, 1999).

He lists six benefits of team-developed assessments.

1. Team-developed common assessments are more efficient.

2. Team-developed common assessments are more equitable.

3. Team-developed common formative assessments are more effective in monitoring and improving student learning.

4. Team-developed common formative assessments can *inform and improve* the practice of both individual teachers and teams of teachers.

5. Team-developed common formative assessments can build the capacity of the team to achieve at higher levels.

6. Team-developed common formative assessments are essential to systematic interventions when students do not learn. (DuFour, 1999)

Once you organize your staff to write the questions, there are some common guidelines to follow:

■ The number of questions needs to be enough to get valid and reliable data—usually two or three questions per standard statement. This translates into about twenty to thirty questions.

■ The questions need to assess the standard statement at the same depth of knowledge as written.

■ The assessment needs to have the same language/vocabulary as the state assessment.

■ The assessment needs to parallel the format of the state assessment. For instance, if the state assessment does not have true-false questions, yours should not have true-false questions.

■ The assessment needs to reflect the blueprint of the state assessment in types of questions. For example, if the state assessment has two-thirds multiple choice and one-third constructed response, create your assessment to have the same ratio.

The assessment team starts by going through the pacing guide, standard by standard, and creating questions that accurately measure the CCSS. Sometimes this might be a single question; other times two or three questions might be necessary to determine mastery. But the team should at least write as many questions as standards listed on the pacing guide.

In *Education Up Close: Writing Effective Tests: A Guide for Teachers*, Glencoe (2005) provides additional guidelines to think about when writing effective assessments, as shown in Figure 3. 4.

Most common formative assessments have multiple-choice and/or constructed-response questions. Writing a constructed-response question is usually the easier of the two to develop; however, it is the hardest to grade with reliability. When writing constructed-response questions, be

- **Figure 3.4** Tips for Writing Effective Assessments

Guideline	Reason
Avoid confusing students with too many negatives in a question. (e.g., What might not have happened had the Allies not won the war?)	Unless they appear on a grammar or logic test, these items rarely test content knowledge. They also may skew the test unfairly toward native English speakers and highly proficient readers.
Avoid using incomplete sentences.	This type of question may provide grammatical clues to the correct answer.
Avoid using "all of the above" as a choice.	Students can easily eliminate this answer by identifying just one incorrect answer.
Write all answer choices to be approximately the same length.	Correct answers are often the longest.
Adjust the level of the question to the level of thinking required to answer it. For example: A simple memorization task: In what year was the Declaration of Independence signed? a. 1770 b. 1876 c. 1776 d. 1786	

A task that requires higher-order thinking skills:
 	
What later historical events best affirm the ideas set forth in the Declaration of Independence?
   a. Emancipation Declaration, 19th Amendment
   b. Eminent Domain, Manifest Destiny
   c. Civil War, World War I
	You can measure higher-order thinking skills by the way you word a question.

Proofread all items before copying the test.	Typographical errors are more often made in incorrect answers and may be apparent to test-wise students.

Source: Glencoe (2005)

aware of the point a response earns. The parts of the question delineate the number of points earned. In other words, if you have a two-point constructed-response question, two clear parts of the question are necessary. An example to illustrate this point is this:

Describe the properties of a metamorphic rock (worth two points).

Although some might think this is a difficult question and a correct answer should be weighed more than a single point, it does not have two clearly separate parts for the student to respond to. The question may easily be rewritten to make it a two-part question with each part worth a point:

Describe the properties of a metamorphic rock and provide a specific example of one (worth two points).

In this question there are clearly two parts, with a point being assigned to each. And though the first part of the explanation might be longer and more time consuming than simply providing a single-word answer, the two parts are weighed equally. The answer sheet for teachers to use when grading provides guidance on acceptable answers and how each point is earned.

An example of a four-point question that covers the same CCSS is the following:

Describe the properties of a metamorphic rock and an igneous rock. Explain how an igneous rock may change into a metamorphic rock. Provide an example of an igneous rock that changes into a metamorphic rock (worth four points).

Provide a rubric for grading such a question, with the team deciding how the points will be distributed. It would look something like this:

■ One point for description of properties of a metamorphic rock

■ One point for description of properties of an igneous rock

■ One point for explanation of how an igneous rock changes into a metamorphic rock

■ One point for an example of an igneous rock that changes into a metamorphic rock

Writing multiple-choice questions may seem easier, but they can be difficult to write to the level of knowledge the standard requires for a student to demonstrate mastery. If the standard you are trying to assess is at an application level, the question must be written at that level as well. A good way to ensure that the question is written at the same level is to use the same verb the CCSS uses. For instance, take this language arts kindergarten vocabulary standard:

> Sort common objects into categories (e.g., shapes, foods) to gain
> a sense of the concepts the categories represent.

A simple question to measure this standard is the following, using the same verb, *sort*:

> Sort the following objects into three equal categories, and create
> a label for each of the categories (two points).
>
> | | |
> |---|---|
> | dog | tennis racquet |
> | pizza | cookies |
> | banana | cat |
> | baseball | hamster |
> | hockey puck | basketball |
> | bird | sandwich |

Make clear in the rubric that the first point is for sorting the objects into the three groups, and the second point is for correctly labeling the categories.

One strategy for writing an effective multiple-choice question is to write it first as a constructed response and then adapt it to multiple choice. An example would be this math Common Core State Standard in third-grade measurement and data:

> Tell and write time to the nearest minute, and measure time
> intervals in minutes.

Writing a constructed response using the verb *write* looks something like this:

> Using the clock provided, write the time to the nearest minute. What time will it be 13 minutes after that?

This question has two parts and addresses the standard. A student who gets it correct shows mastery of that CCSS. This constructed response can be adapted into two multiple-choice questions that also accurately measure the standard:

> Using the clock provided, what is the time to the nearest minute when the class started the math assignment?
>
>   a. 1:15 p.m.
>
>   b. 3:03 p.m.
>
>   c. 3:05 p.m.
>
>   d. 4:03 p.m.
>
> The students finished the assignment in thirteen minutes. What time did they finish?
>
>   a. 1:28
>
>   b. 3:16
>
>   c. 3:18
>
>   d. 4:16

This is a fairly basic adaptation. Sometimes multiple-choice questions take more creativity. Take this constructed-response question from the CCSS reading standards for literacy grades 9–10:

> Compare the point of view of the two authors on the next page and how they treat the same topic. Which of the authors presents a better case, and what evidence supports your judgment?

Selection 1	Selection 2
Although the measure of humans' impact on global warming isn't precisely known, scientific evidence makes it abundantly clear that human activity is the main cause of warming over the past several decades. Natural drivers of climate simply cannot account for the recent dramatic increase in the Earth's temperature. Human activity, especially burning fossil fuels and clearing forests, contributes to carbon dioxide in the air. The CO_2 acts like a thick blanket, trapping heat that would otherwise escape into space. If we are going to prevent the worst consequences of global warming—increased risks of drought, more widespread heat waves and rising sea levels—we have to act now to limit the amount of CO_2 we put into the atmosphere. We need federal action to limit heat-trapping emissions, and we need it now. Solutions for cutting emissions are abundant, affordable and have other benefits that make them worthy of consideration regardless of climate impact. Mandating higher fuel efficiency for automobiles will make our nation less dependent on foreign oil, protect auto industry jobs, and save money for consumers. Investing in renewable energy will drive down utility costs, create more jobs than other power sources, and provide a clean way to generate electricity. Global warming is a human problem, but that means we humans can all do something about it. —Brenda Ekwurzel	Record snowfall illustrates the obvious: The global warming fraud is without equal in modern science. The fundamental problems exposed about climate-change theory undermine the very basis of scientific inquiry. Huge numbers of researchers refuse to provide their data to other scientists. Some referenced data is found not to have existed. The U.N. Intergovernmental Panel on Climate Change 2007 reported that global warming activists continually cite invented a large number of purported facts. Consider a few of the problems with the U.N. report that came to light over the past few weeks. ♦ The Himalayan glaciers were supposed to disappear as soon as 2035. The United Nations didn't base this hysteria on an academic study. Instead, it relied on a news story that interviewed a single Indian glaciologist in 1999. Syed Hasnain, the glaciologist in question, says he was misquoted and provided no date to the reporter. The doomsday account was simply made up, and the United Nations never bothered to confirm the claim. ♦ Because of purported global warming, the world supposedly "suffered rapidly rising costs due to extreme weather-related events since the 1970s." The U.N. cited one unpublished study to prove this. When the research eventually was published in 2008 after the IPCC report was released, the authors backpedaled: "We find insufficient evidence to claim a statistical relationship between global temperature increase and catastrophe losses." ♦ Up to 40 percent of the Amazon rain forest was said to be at risk because of rising global temperatures. Again, the U.N. didn't cite any academic studies but merely one non-refereed report authored by two non-scientists, one of whom worked for the World Wildlife Fund, an activist organization. ♦ The U.N. dramatically claimed that 55 percent of the Netherlands is below sea level when the accurate portion is 26 percent. Man-made global warming theory isn't backed up by science; it's a hoax. The fact that the world has been asked to spend tens of trillions of dollars on global warming solutions without being able to evaluate the data upon which the claims were made should have been the first warning that something was seriously wrong. The public and world leaders have been sold expensive snake oil by charlatans. —The *Washington Post*

Students have to read both passages and analyze the differences between the two opinions. Because the opinions are not blatantly stated, students have to discern the information from the passages. They also have to evaluate which of the two selections presents the better case, citing specific examples from the passages to support their opinion. Here are two examples of how this could be turned into a multiple-choice question:

What is the main difference in the point of view of the two authors?

   a. One think humans cause global warming, and the other thinks nature does.

   b. One thinks global warming can be stopped, and the other does not.

   c. One thinks global warming is a problem, and the other believes it is a hoax.

   d. One thinks the measure of human impact on global warming is clear, and the other thinks it is not.

Which of the following is a strong argument for which of the authors presents the better case?

   a. One presents the case with more passion.

   b. One presents more specific examples to back the point of view.

   c. One uses too much opinion.

   d. One cites more examples for how to fix the problem.

The second multiple-choice question does not allow students to form their own opinions, but it does lead them to evaluate which of the choices presents a better case, making it an evaluation-level question. For further hints on writing multiple-choice questions, the Principal's Office includes a summary of suggestions for writing multiple-choice questions provided by the education department at the University of Indiana (page 91).

Answer to Formative Assessment Question #4: Why is it important that common formative assessments be both reliable and valid?

Having common formative assessments that are both reliable and valid is important so the data from the assessments will be accurate. Knowing that the test is measuring the performance of students on an equal playing field is crucial. For example, a student who passes the formative assessment in Mrs. Brown's class is showing the same level of mastery as a student who passes the assessment in Mr. Thompson's class. As for being valid, if you believe a question is testing a student on the mastery of a CCSS and it actually is not, you are giving the student credit for something he or she has not yet grasped; that is when students begin to fall through the cracks. The validity comes in that a question is measuring the CCSS it was intended to, giving you an accurate picture of what a student has and has not mastered.

You need both reliable and valid assessments because if the data you collect is not accurate, the adjustments you make to the school will not have the effects you wish them to have. It would be like treating a patient who has a cold with a cast. You are not matching the treatment with the ailment.

Answer to Formative Assessment Question #5: How will the SCORE Process provide professional development for a teaching staff?

Going through the SCORE Process as a staff acts as professional development. The conversations and collaboration that occur among staff member allows them to learn from one another, whether it be an understanding of the CCSS, an analysis of the state test itself, or the writing of the common formative assessments. It would certainly be easier to have someone do all this work and write the assessments and just give it to your teachers; however, the valuable professional development would be lost. Most important, this process will make your staff members better teachers because they will be more familiar with the CCSS and will be better at forming their own questions to use in their day-to-day teaching as well as on their own formative assessments.

chapter four

Creating the Assessment Environment

Good management is the art of making problems so interesting and their solutions so constructive that everyone wants to get to work and deal with them (Hawken, 2010).

Now that team members have designed the assessments, they can take the next step in the SCORE Process—administering the assessment. See Figure 4.1 (page 44).

Common formative assessments provide four distinct benefits—the four Es.

Exposure: To give students planned and purposeful *exposure* to the standards and assessment format

Expertise: To develop *expertise* in each teacher's ability to ask higher-level questions, base instructional decisions for delivery on performance data, and collaborate for curricular direction across grade levels

Endurance: To build *endurance* for each student to have the stamina to sit for long periods of time as well as to work through difficult questions

Empower: To *empower* students and their parents to become responsible decision makers for learning

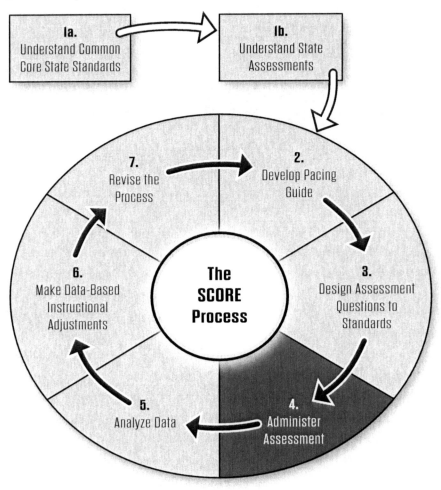

Figure 4.1 Step Four in the SCORE Process

1a.
Understand Common Core State Standards

1b.
Understand State Assessments

7. Revise the Process

2. Develop Pacing Guide

6. Make Data-Based Instructional Adjustments

The SCORE Process

3. Design Assessment Questions to Standards

5. Analyze Data

4. Administer Assessment

Exposure has been accomplished through instruction aligned to the pacing guide. Intentionally teaching the CCSS in a systematic way provides an assurance that students are taught the standards and not just the interests of the teacher. The **expertise** of the teacher has been increased through the work on the common assessments, from the analysis of the CCSS and assessments to the writing of the actual assessment questions.

Testing the **endurance** of students is addressed by administering the assessments in a purposeful manner. The common formative assessments your teaching staff administers need to be an organized effort that models the state testing process as much as possible. This is part of the exposure to the test. If students are comfortable with testing conditions and become familiar with them, they will not be overwhelmed when the state assessments are given. This is a substantial advantage for the students.

One aspect that can mask the true abilities of students on an assessment is test anxiety. Students are so nervous about the actual test, they make silly mistakes and do not perform commensurate with their skill levels. Preparing students for high-stakes testing is important because they face it the rest of their academic careers, from year-end achievement tests to college entrance exams to licensure as doctors, lawyers, and teachers. If students feel as though formative assessments are a part of the regular school environment, they will be more relaxed when taking them and, as a result, give you more accurate data on what they know and understand.

Conveying the Message

One of the most important factors in the success of the SCORE Process lies within the attitude of the teachers who administer the assessments. Nothing hampers the testing process more than teachers who do not take the assessments and administration of them seriously. A teacher's attitude is contagious. Through the training conducted in the creation of the pacing guide and common formative assessments, staff members should be very familiar with and see the advantages of using the SCORE Process. If you do not feel they are properly informed of these advantages or if the entire staff was not part of the process of creating the formative assessments, some professional development concerning the advantages of common formative assessments might be necessary to put everyone on the same page. An outline for a staff meeting session that informs the staff of the benefits of common formative assessments is provided in the Principal's Office (page 94).

Teachers often underestimate the power they have to influence students, not only in the day-to-day working of the classroom but also in the very important world of test taking. As the school leader, you must stress this importance to staff members and remind them that when a teacher goes in with the attitude of "I really do not want to give this test; it is only going to take away from valuable class time," students easily sense it and carry the attitude into their performance on the assessment. That is why it is key to be consistent in the administration of the common formative assessments. Make sure teachers are up front with the students about the rationale for taking formative assessments and how the data will be used to guide instruction. The school leader needs to make sure every staff member understands this rationale and knows how to convey it clearly. Students who understand the importance of the tests try their best and show where they are in understanding the CCSS.

Make sure to explain to students that if they have a poor showing on the common formative assessments, the material will probably need to be retaught. This could motivate them to take the testing more seriously. Keep in mind that students will take the assessment only as seriously as the staff does, so be sure to discuss with teachers.

If you want to make sure that the message is clear and consistent, have an assembly with students and convey this message as school leader. Schools often get the student body together for sporting events, concerts, or other extracurricular activities, but rarely do schools assemble students to talk about student achievement. Your assembly need not be boring, where you talk *at* the students, but something demonstrating the importance of the assessments. You could have students create and act out humorous skits about taking the common formative assessment and what happens when one student does not take it seriously. Or you could challenge students with incentives meant to inspire them to perform their best. Nothing gets students more excited about assessments than the possibility of duct-taping the school leader to the wall or throwing a pie in the face of a certain teacher.

To Review or Not to Review?

One aspect of formative assessments that differs from summative assessments that you should stress to your staff is that no study guide or review is used with formative assessments. The goal is to figure out if students have enduring understanding of the skills and have actually learned. If teachers review with students right before the formative assessment or provide them with a review guide, students will not necessarily show what they have mastered. Instead, they may recall the information from the review that was just provided. Remember, the expectation is enduring understanding of skills and knowledge.

This aspect of the common formative assessment process is not comfortable for some teachers. Review may be part of good instructional practice the teachers use. Teachers may feel compelled to give students whatever advantage they can because they feel these assessments are a reflection of their teaching ability. The school leader must help the teaching staff understand and feel comfortable with the idea that these assessments are about gathering information, not giving students, or teachers, a grade. That means the good, the bad, and the ugly.

It may help to think of this part of the process in the following way: Suppose you take your car in for its final checkup just before the warranty expires. Would you want your mechanic to temporarily fix the things that are wrong with your car so that a couple of months later it breaks down and you are stuck with an expensive repair bill? Of course not. You would want to know what is wrong with your car before the warranty runs out, so problems can be fixed without any cost to you. The same goes for the students. The staff needs to address student skill deficiencies prior to the state assessment, before students are held accountable in their achievement. The common formative assessment is still a time to catch problems with no consequences to the students, staff, or school.

Remember the goal is to see what students truly understand and expose any gaps there might be in enduring understanding of CCSS. The school leader wants all the warts and blemishes to appear on this common formative assessment. Then something can be done about them.

Creating the Environment

The school leader wields a powerful tool in creating the proper testing environment: the PA system. If you are the voice that comes on to deliver the morning or afternoon announcements, the message you give students can set the tone for the entire school. The seriousness with which you take the assessments trickles down through staff and students.

During the week leading up to the common formative assessments, you might include a test tip of the day in the announcements to remind students of little things they can do to show their true ability on the assessments. These are simple things such as taking their time, making sure to have a good breakfast before the assessment, and getting to school on time. The Principal's Office contains a list of several other possible test-taking hints (page 100).

Another simple way to set the environment is to put up inspirational signs to show students how seriously the school is taking the common formative assessments. The signs can be purchased from teacher stores, printed to make them specific to your school, or even created by students. Here are some examples:

> **At this school, we do things the _write_ way.**
>
> **Do your best on constructed responses.**

> Think before you bubble. We want to know just how smart you are!

> **2 points means**
>
> **2 parts to the question.**
>
> **Read the questions carefully.**

> Use your #2 pencil to show you are #1.

Post signs in hallways, classrooms, and even the entrance to the school so that the first thing students and visitors to the school see is how seriously the school is taking the common formative assessments.

Mimicking the State Assessment Schedule

On the actual day or week of the testing, administer the common formative assessments purposefully. View the testing as a dress rehearsal. In a proper dress rehearsal, everything is done in the exact same manner as in the final performance. Actors wear the costumes and speak their lines loudly, stage-hands move the scenery—cast members are put through everything they will experience during a live show; the only difference is that there is no audience to judge them. Similarly, the only thing that should be different in the common formative assessment experience compared to the year-end state assessment is the lack of judgment. Instead, the common assessments are used to help students when the final performance comes about.

Here are some things to consider for administering your common formative assessments:

- How does the state administer its tests?
  - □ Two in a day, one a day, all in a single week, spread out over two weeks?

- Is everyone on board? Does everyone know the plan?

- Do the assessments have directions consistent with state assessments?

- Does the regular school schedule need to be altered?

- Have the proper people (administrators, specials teachers, lunchroom staff) been notified?
  - □ Are the room arrangements similar to the setup students will experience with the state tests?

- Do some students require accommodations?
  - □ Have you arranged help for students who need the test read to them or need someone to write for them

- Are some grade levels or teachers not taking part in the assessment?
  - □ Are they aware of the process, and will they make sure the noise level in their classrooms and hallways will not be distracting?

For the proper environment, everything from the morning announcements to the restroom schedule to the classroom setup should be the same as for the year-end assessment. For instance, if during the state assessments, students are seated no more than twenty to a room and must sign out to use the restroom, the same should be true during the common formative assessment. If the state assessment has a time limit, which most of them do, then the same type of time limit should be established for the common formative assessment. Since this is a shorter assessment without as many questions, an appropriate time limit needs to be determined. For instance, if your state allots sixty minutes to take the full science test, then a time limit of thirty minutes may be appropriate for a partial assessment. This serves to get students used to managing their time and not getting stuck on any one question, developing better test-taking strategies.

Because you are unfolding these formative assessments as an entire school, it is important that groups be consistent. All teachers giving the math assessment at a certain grade level should give it on the same day and at the same time. When the schedule is drawn up, it should model the state schedule as well. For instance, if the school usually gives the state writing assessment in the morning, all the language arts teachers should do the same with their common formative assessments. Most states provide a window of time and allow the district to decide how to administer the tests. A schedule might look like this:

	Monday	Tuesday	Wednesday	Thursday	Friday
Week 1	5th/7th Reading	6th/8th Reading	5th/7th Math	6th/8th Math	
Week 2	5th Science	7th Science	5th Social Studies	7th Social Studies	

You might consider staggering the schedule much like this example. This builds student endurance in small quantities so that once students have gone through this process for three or four cycles, they will be ready for the state assessment at year's end.

Things as simple as making sure the hallways are quiet and that there are no interruptions in the classroom or announcements disrupting student focus are important. Posting a sign outside classroom doors, so people do not enter, is a small thing that goes a long way. There is a sign in the Principal's Office (page 101) that can be copied and posted on doors.

The materials students are allowed to use also need to be consistent. If the state assessment allows students to use calculators, students should be allowed to do so on the common formative assessments. On the converse side, if calculators are not permitted, the same goes for formative assessments. It is important to find out what the state does and does not allow or provide for at each grade level and emulate those conditions.

Making directions consistent and clear is also crucial to the positive testing environment. Every teacher should read the same set of directions and run the classroom the same way. This will take a certain amount of coordination but will be extremely beneficial to the students to help them develop a routine with assessments, thus helping them develop exposure to the test. Sample test directions are included in the Principal's Office (page 102).

Answer to Formative Assessment Question #6: What are the two most important factors when administering common formative assessments?

When administering the common formative assessments to a building, the school leader should focus on two factors: (1) setting the proper environment, with positive messages that the school is taking the assessments seriously and thus so should the students, and (2) administering and modeling the assessments consistently. Teachers and students should get the consistent message that the common formative assessments are going to improve student achievement. The role of the school leader is to be a consistent voice and stay on point with that central message. As a result, the data will be more useful for instructional implications.

chapter five

Organizing and Using Data Effectively

If all students are expected to demonstrate the same knowledge and skills, regardless of the teacher to which they are assigned, it only makes sense that teachers must work together in a collaborative effort to assess student learning (DuFour, DuFour, Eaker, & Many, 2010).

*I*t would be a shame to follow the SCORE Process, studying the CCSS and state assessments, creating a pacing guide, and meticulously writing the questions for your assessments, only to lose some reliability due to inter-rater reliability during grading. So far, we have used the word *consistency* often in the SCORE Process. This consistency should continue in the grading of the common formative assessments.

Being consistent in the grading of the common formative assessments is imperative to ensure usable data with which to make instructional decisions. Everyone who grades the assessments should award points consistently for the constructed responses. Having a tough teacher give a student two points out of four on a constructed response, while a more lenient teacher awards three points for the same response skews the assessment results and makes them unreliable. One point may not seem like much, but if there are multiple constructed responses, points add up.

Providing collaboration time around anchor grading is a good way to provide this consistency. Anchoring is a systematic and reliable process for grading assessments and provides guidance to teachers when grading constructed-response items.

Anchoring consists of several people grading the same assessment, with the same scoring guide and exemplars, and determining how many points the student earned. After each person grades the assessment, the scores are compared among the group. If the assessment is perfectly anchored and reliable, every grader will have the same score. If there are some divergent scores, teachers discuss how they graded the item until a consensus is reached. Scoring guides and exemplars may be revised or added to, accommodating the new information gained through this process. It is important to have a few rounds of anchoring and discussion to set the standard for what type of student response earns the different levels of points available. A team of teachers may act as the graders—all the teachers in a given subject area or even an entire teaching staff. A benefit of anchoring together as a staff is that teachers have conversations about teaching and learning. What constitutes a proper response for a particular standard? Does it lead to discussion about the content standard itself? These conversations provide authentic learning opportunities for teachers to learn from one another.

We conducted one session of anchor grading with an entire school staff, including specials teachers. Teachers were grading the math assessment, which had been written by the high school math teachers, with an answer key the math teachers had developed as well. They had probably looked at this assessment and answer key a hundred times between them all. Yet when the assessment was put in front of one of the home economics teachers, she glanced at it and said, "This key is wrong." Sure enough, the math teachers had done the math wrong, and no one had caught it until then. If the home economics teacher had not seen the error, the question would have been scored incorrectly, and the data would have been skewed.

Another approach for anchor grading is to project an example of student responses for all to see, and have teachers discuss how they would grade the responses, with the answer key in front of them. The group establishes student examples for all point levels. For instance, if the question is a four-point question, teachers should establish zero-, one-, two-, three-, and four-point examples. Doing a couple of examples is helpful to guide graders. Anchor grading also facilitates more discussion among the staff.

No matter what method is used to grade the assessments, it is important that the grading be done anonymously. Teachers should not see the names of students or grade students they work with directly. Grading in this way ensures that the inherent bias teachers have of their students, whether good or bad, does not factor into the grading.

Organizing the Data

The data from your formative assessments gives you information that is

- instant
- simple
- usable

This data is instant; there is no sending it away and waiting a couple of months before seeing the results. The results are available as soon as teachers grade and analyze them. The data from the common formative assessments is very simple. In some cases, it shows that students either master the skill or do not. There is no interpretation of numbers or figuring out a complex formula. Teachers get the score, compare it to others, analyze the reasons for any deviations, and determine what actions need to take place in the classroom. Usability is a very important aspect of the data. Teachers get a lot of information on their students, but how much of it are they actually able to use? Teachers can determine classroom adjustments based on the data from the common formative assessments.

That leads to step five in the SCORE Process, data analysis (see Figure 5.1, page 56).

Before you can analyze the data, you must figure out a way to organize it to make it useful to those looking at it. Here are a few suggestions for simple ways to organize the student data so that it can be properly analyzed.

Class Profile Graph

The class profile graph, like its namesake, profiles every student in the class who took the assessment and how each scored. By gathering this information, you can determine whether a majority of your students are "getting it" and which ones specifically are not. Figure 5.2 (page 57) is an example of a class profile graph. It lists every student in the class on the X axis and his or her percentage score on the Y axis to chart how individual students performed on the common formative assessment.

Figure 5.1 Step Five in the SCORE Process

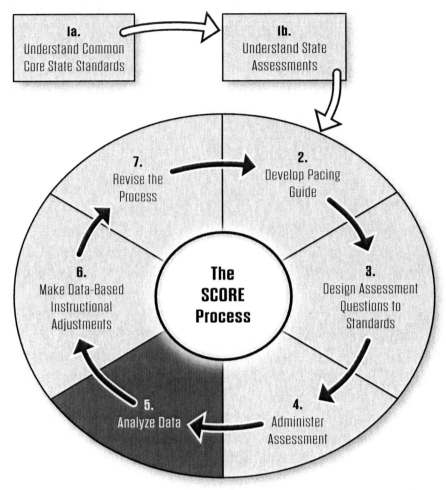

Such a graph can pinpoint which individual students need intervention. For instance, in the example shown in Figure 5.2, Student #1 is performing lower than peers, so you might need to differentiate by reteaching certain topics or offering additional help to that student. This graph can also allow teaching staff to make sure student achievement and student ability match each other. Students should not have more than a standard deviation between their classroom grade and their formative assessment score. In other words, students who receive a B in a math class should not score any lower than a C on the math common formative assessment. If a student does, then classroom achievement is not commensurate with the common formative assessment. Similarly, if a student is getting a D in

· **Figure 5.2** Class Profile Graph Example

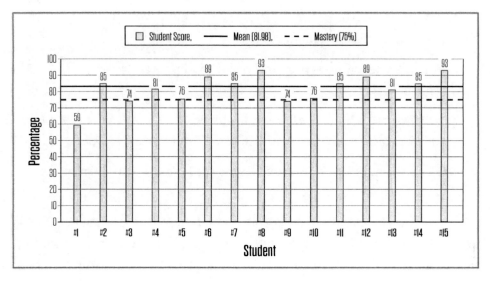

language arts class, a red flag should go up if he or she receives a B on the language arts common formative assessment. Somehow an accurate skill level is not being reflected in the class.

In analyzing the class profile graph, teachers should look for patterns that make sense. When student achievement and ability do not match, they should look for answers in the data. For example, "Johnny" scores eighty-five percent on the common formative assessment but is failing the class. Using this data, his teacher investigates to find out why there is a discrepancy. Possible reasons are the following:

- Johnny does not do his homework regularly, which pulls his grades down.

- His attendance or behavior causes a lower grade.

- He may be embarrassed socially to do well in class, so he underachieves.

- Perhaps a poor home life prevents him from reaching his potential.

- One grade may be pulling down his average.

Another important aspect when analyzing data is to look for trends. If "Marisol" performs poorly in comparison to her previous achievement, and this is something new, there could be several factors involved:

- Marisol may suffer from text anxiety.

- She may have bubbled in the wrong number once, throwing the sequence off on the answer form.

- She may be a poor writer and performed poorly on the constructed-response questions, pulling down the results.

- She may be a hard worker who achieves high grades because of this but lacks enduring understanding of standard skills.

- She may not have been feeling well the day of the assessment or forgot to have breakfast.

These are all possible roads of investigation to pursue while tracking down the reason for an unexpected poor performance on a formative assessment. The class profile graph allows the teacher to pinpoint any anomalies to the individual student. Directions on creating a class profile graph and a blank template are in the Principal's Office (pages 104–106).

Classroom Item Analysis Graph

The classroom item analysis graph (Figure 5.3) charts each question from the assessment with the overall average of how the class performed on it. The X axis displays each question identified by number, standard, and even format if desired. The Y axis represents the score of percent mastered. Because this is a mastery graph, it is important to remember that on a one-point multiple-choice question, the student needs to get the question correct to earn mastery. At the same time, on a multi-point constructed-response question, the student needs to score at least seventy-five percent, or three out of four on a four-point question or three out of three on a three-point question. Scoring a two out of four on a four-point question would be only fifty percent, far from mastery.

To analyze the data on this particular report, teachers look for the low-scoring questions and try to discern a pattern. For instance, on Figure 5.3, students did very poorly on question 2. Obviously, the teacher wants to know why. Is it because the question was a short answer and students struggled with those? Was this particular standard one that was not taught as well as it could have been? Maybe the question itself was not well written, and students were confused. Another possible pattern involves

· **Figure 5.3** Classroom Item Analysis Graph

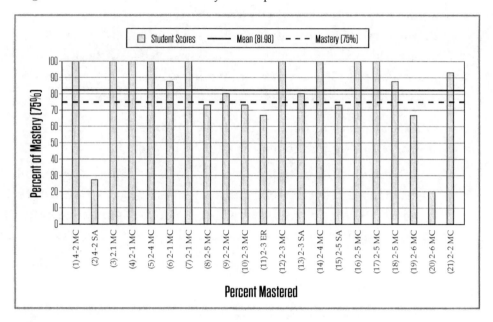

questions 19 and 20, both from standard 2-6. Overall, students did not do well on this standard, which shows it was not taught at a mastery level and probably needs to be retaught.

Here are some other patterns we have seen when analyzing common formative assessments and some suggestions for improvement:

- **Pattern:** Most of the lower-scoring questions are constructed-response questions, in which students have to write their responses.

  - □ **Instructional implication:** students need more exposure to multipart questions and writing.

- **Pattern:** Most of the lower-scoring questions relate to higher-level standards.

  - □ **Instructional implication:** students need more exposure to higher-level questions in the classroom.

- **Pattern:** Most of the higher-scoring questions are lower-level, multiple choice.

  - □ **Instructional implication:** students need continued exposure to these types of questions because they are the building blocks for the higher-level questions.

- **Pattern:** Lower-scoring questions are from the same standard category (for example, in math, probability).

  - ☐ **Instructional implication:** This may be a standard that is not a strength for the teacher. All teachers have strengths and weaknesses. The key is figuring out a way around a weakness through professional development or collaboration.

- **Pattern:** Higher-scoring questions are from the same standard category (for example, in math, patterns).

  - ☐ **Instructional implication:** This may be a standard that is taught often in the provided textbook/materials. Students may need to spend less time on this standard, as it may be taking time away from a standard with which students have more difficulty.

- **Pattern:** Higher-scoring questions are at the beginning of the assessment, and lower-scoring questions are at the end.

  - ☐ **Instructional implication:** students need to work on one of two things or maybe both: (1) endurance in taking a test, giving the same effort at the end of the test as at the beginning, (2) pacing during the test; they may have run out of time and left questions at the end blank.

Many times the classroom item analysis graph indicates questions that need to be revised on the common formative assessments because they are written poorly and cause confusion or result in mistakes. However, a question should not be revised to make it easier because a majority of the students missed it. Teachers who feel the urge to do this should determine if the question was truly fair. If it was, then they should examine how the standard was taught. Often teachers want to change the question rather than the instruction. This does not help the students, which is what the entire process is about.

Directions and a blank template for creating a classroom item analysis graph are in the Principal's Office (pages 107–108).

Non-Mastery Report

The non-mastery report (Figure 5.4) is a combination of the class profile graph and the classroom item analysis graph. It lists students who did not master a particular question and groups them by the CCSS. To develop a non-mastery report, teachers list each question and which students did not master that particular question.

The value of such a report is in the ability to figure out flexible grouping for differentiated instruction. When a teacher sees that four students missed question #10 and the standard needs to be retaught, just those students can be grouped, without wasting the time of other students who mastered that particular standard. Question #11 had six students who did not master the question. The question was an extended response, so the teachers need to determine whether it was a content issue or whether the students struggled because the question required a written answer. Once they figure that

• **Figure 5.4** Non-Mastery Report

Question 9, Standard-GLI: 2-2, Multiple Choice
Explain how almost all kinds of animals' food can be traced back to plants.

Student #1	
Student #7	
Student #13	

Question 10, Standard-GLI: 2-3, Multiple Choice
Trace the organization of simple food chains and food webs (e.g., producers, herbivores, carnivores, omnivores, and decomposers).

Student #1	Student #6
Student #4	Student #15

Question 11, Standard-GLI: 2-3, Extended Response
Trace the organization of simple food chains and food webs (e.g., producers, herbivores, carnivores, omnivores, and decomposers).

Student #1	Student #7
Student #2	Student #8
Student #5	Student #13

Question 12, Standard-GLI: 2-3, Multiple Choice
Trace the organization of simple food chains and food webs (e.g., producers, herbivores, carnivores, omnivores, and decomposers).

Question 13, Standard-GLI: 2-3, Short Answer
Trace the organization of simple food chains and food webs (e.g., producers, herbivores, carnivores, omnivores, and decomposers).

Student #3	Student #12	Student #7
Student #4	Student #13	Student #9
Student #11	Student #6	Student #10

out, the teachers can provide the proper instruction to help this group of students achieve mastery. Most of the class did not master question #13, so that standard most likely needs to be retaught to the entire class.

The non-mastery report gives teachers a good idea where they need to differentiate without creating permanent groups. Flexible grouping is necessary in the classroom not only to move students at different levels but also to place emphasis on different content areas according to the needs of the students. An A student does not necessarily master everything, and someone who is failing is capable of mastering some things. Directions and a blank template for a non-mastery report are in the Principal's Office (pages 109–110).

Student Report

A more personalized way to break down the data is in a student report (Figure 5.5). It is an individualized report showing each student and correct questions, missed questions, and the areas that need work.

Notice that student #1 did not master nine of the questions (indicated by the N). This in itself is a red flag, but even more telling is that four of these are constructed responses, which indicates student #1 might be struggling with the written part of the assessment. Teachers would want to figure out interventions that could help this student with that aspect. Student #2 on the other hand missed only three questions. There is not a cause for concern, not only because of the low number but also because the CCSS student #2 did not master, 4-2, 2-3, and 2-6, were mastered on other questions dealing with that standard.

Organizing the data can help three sets of people:

1. The student can see what he or she was successful at and what needs work.

2. The parents can be given this report at a parent-teacher conference, or it can be sent home so that they can see what their child needs to work on.

3. Supplemental teachers, such as study hall teachers or tutors, can see what they need to work on with the student and what successful skills can be built upon.

Figure 5.5 Student Report

Student One

5th Grade 4th 9 Weeks Science — Stanley

Standard-GLI	4-2	2-1	2-1	2-4	2-1	2-1	2-5	2-3	2-2	2-3	2-3	2-3	2-4	2-5	2-5	2-5	2-5	2-6	2-6	2-2	Total	Percent
Point Value	2	1	1	1	1	1	1	1	1	4	1	1	1	1	1	1	1	1	1	1	16	59.26
Question	2	3	4	5	6	7	8	9	10	11	12	13	14	15	16	17	18	19	20	21		
Score	1	1	1	1	1	1	0	0	0	2	1	1	1	0	1	1	0	1	0	1		
Stud. Ans.	-	-	-	-	-	-	0	0	-	-	-	-	-	-	-	-	0	-	0	-		
Non-mastery	N						N	N	N			N		N			N		N			

Student needs work on the following

Grade.Standard.GLI	GLI Description
5.2.2	Explain how almost all kinds of animals' food can be traced back to plants.
5.2.3	Trace the organization of simple food chains and food webs (e.g., producers, herbivores, carnivores, omnivores, and decomposers).
5.2.5	Support how an organism's patterns of behavior are related to the nature of that organism's ecosystem, including the kinds and numbers of other organisms present, the availability of food and resources, and the changing physical characteristics of the ecosystem.
5.2.6	Analyze how organisms, including humans, cause changes in their ecosystems and how these changes can be beneficial, natural, or detrimental (e.g., beaver ponds, earthworm burrows, grasshoppers eating plants, people planting and cutting trees, and people introducing a new species.
5.4.2	Revise an existing design used to solve a problem based on peer review.

Student Two

5th Grade 4th 9 Weeks Science — Stanley

Standard-GLI	4-2	2-1	2-1	2-4	2-1	2-1	2-5	2-3	2-2	2-3	2-3	2-3	2-4	2-5	2-5	2-5	2-5	2-6	2-6	2-2	Total	Percent
Point Value	2	1	1	1	1	1	1	1	1	4	1	1	1	2	1	1	1	1	1	1	16	59.26
Question	2	3	4	5	6	7	8	9	10	11	12	13	14	15	16	17	18	19	20	21		
Score	1	1	1	1	1	1	1	1	1	0	3	1	1	2	1	1	1	1	0	1		
Stud. Ans.	-	-	-	-	-	-	-	-	-	3	-	-	-	2	-	-	-	1	0	-		
Non-mastery	N									N									N			

Student needs work on the following

Grade.Standard.GLI	GLI Description
5.2.3	Trace the organization of simple food chains and food webs (e.g., producers, herbivores, carnivores, omnivores, and decomposers).
5.2.6	Analyze how organisms, including humans, cause changes in their ecosystems and how these changes can be beneficial, natural, or detrimental (e.g., beaver ponds, earthworm burrows, grasshoppers eating plants, people planting and cutting trees, and people introducing a new species.
5.4.2	Revise an existing design used to solve a problem based on peer review.

A good way to use the student report is to arrange conferences at which the teacher and student can talk one-on-one about what the student did well and what could be improved upon. This teaches the student to analyze his or her data and empowers the student, the fourth E of the four Es.

Improving Student Achievement

Now that teachers have collected the data and organized it, they can begin to analyze to properly inform instruction, step six in the SCORE Process (Figure 5.6).

Where are there gaps that need to be filled, or what areas need to be retaught to make sure students have mastery of the topic? This information should be apparent through the data gathered from the common formative assessments.

One approach to analyzing the data is for the staff to have a whole-group discussion to see what patterns emerge from the data. For instance, if the data shows a high number of students struggling with the constructed-response questions, what can the teaching staff do differently to improve this skill? Format more of the day-to-day classroom tests to model constructed responses so students become better practiced at answering them? Or have language arts teachers work with the students to better strategize how to answer constructed-response questions. For any pattern that arises from the data, what strategies can be employed to continue to see the same results or improve student results? As the school leader, make sure to steer the discussions to improvements and instructional implications. Teachers may allow the conversation to be about factors that are completely out of their hands. The school leader should focus on elements that can be controlled within the school environment. As a reminder, Figure 5.7 shows factors that teachers can and cannot control in regard to their students:

Guiding the data meetings and facilitating data discussions is a linchpin in the success of changing the school environment into an effective, successful organization. Organizing and preparing the data meetings and modeling how to extract instructional implications cannot be understated. Moore (2011) describes six steps in the analysis process:

1. Displaying the data in a user-friendly way
2. Asking questions about the data patterns

• **Figure 5.6** Step Six in the SCORE Process

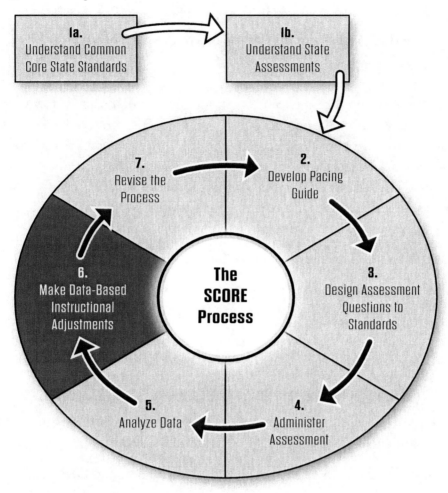

• **Figure 5.7** Factors Teachers Can and Cannot Control

Can Control	Cannot Control
Structure	Home life
High expectations	Self-esteem
Consistency	Lack of sleep
Encouragement	Parent support
Inspiration	Attitude
Materials	Self-motivation
Quiet test-taking environment	Focus

3. Answering questions generated from the data patterns

4. Forming instructional plans implied by the data

5. Making goals to change the results of the data

6. Knowing how to asses these goals

All these steps are the framework for conversations about formative data. It may sound like a lot to do, but when this process is practiced several times, it becomes second nature and the way everyone does school. It also makes better teachers.

Once the teachers have identified patterns that need to be improved and has set goals for improvement, the school leader's next step is to provide support and offer help to achieve this. Some ideas follow:

- Altering the schedule to allow for longer durations of instruction

- Regrouping students into flexible groups of skill mastery for certain standards

- Figuring out ways to allow teachers to co-teach, especially if one teacher is getting great results while another has inconsistent results

- Forming new classes to help with certain CCSS

- Purchasing materials that supplement and support the learning of students

- Offering before- or after-school tutoring for students having difficulty

- Providing time for teacher observation of other teachers

- Scheduling time for professional learning communities around instructional strategies

- Asking follow-up questions and having discussion about how new instructional strategies and interventions are going

- Providing specific feedback on new strategies and interventions observed during classroom visits

- Being visible and enthusiastic about changes and improvements

The staff should be encouraged to analyze the common formative assessments with the students as well. Having the students self-reflect on their results helps them discover both their strengths and their weaknesses. One of the most important skills students can learn is self-awareness or metacognition. Knowing what their strengths and weaknesses are makes them better learners.

Teachers might want to have students reflect as part of a writing assignment. Some of the questions that foster such reflection are these:

- What are my strengths relative to the CCSS?

- What skills have I improved upon over the last grading period?

- Where are my areas of improvement, or what skills do I still need to understand?

- Where didn't I perform as desired, and how might I make my answers better?

- What do these results mean for the next steps in my learning, and how should I prepare for that improvement?

- What types of questions do I need to become more skilled at answering?

All of this leads us into the fourth E in regard to the benefits of common formative assessments:

Empower: To *empower* teachers, students, and parents to become responsible decision makers for learning. Once all stakeholders have reliable and valid data to make sound decisions, all feel empowered to change and grow. Using the data to empower the stakeholders becomes the foundation for change and progress.

Providing teachers with data analysis skills to make data-based decisions changes instruction. Teachers understand how baseline data or formative data is used to set goals and ways to collect data to show improvement. This is where the synergy in the SCORE Process starts. Using data to drive instruction provides the catalyst to keep the cycle moving and progressing.

Teaching students how to become better learners empowers them to become responsible for their own learning. It is important not just to give students their results but also to analyze and synthesize the information; providing students with timely, specific feedback leads to student reflection and growth. All teachers have spent hours grading student responses, writing in meticulous detail how students can improve their efforts and get better results, only to see the students glance at the grade, and then pitch the test in the trash. Teachers have to find effective ways to give students feedback on their formative assessments. Nicol and Macfarlane-Dick (2006) list seven characteristics of high-quality feedback:

1. It clarifies what good performance is (goals, criteria, and expected standards).
2. It facilitates the development of self-assessment in learning.
3. It provides high-quality information to students about their learning.
4. It encourages teacher and peer dialogue around learning.
5. It encourages positive motivational beliefs and self-esteem.
6. It provides opportunities to close the gap between current and desired performance.
7. It provides information to teachers and students that can be used to help shape teaching and learning.

Being able to provide this feedback to students could go a long way toward improving student achievement, which after all, is one of the most important goals.

Another method of empowering is to have a meeting for parents to educate them in how to interpret the information from the common formative assessments. Many times parents are bottom-line people when it comes to the grades of their children. They just want to know whether they have a good grade or not. But knowing how to analyze and break down the results from the common formative assessment empowers parents to be able to assist. This might come in the form of working with their children on a skill the assessment shows they are struggling with or arranging to have a tutor strengthen certain skills. The more the school leader informs and educates the parents, the more empowered they become and the better they will be in assisting the school staff in meeting the needs of their children.

Using Data to Develop Teacher Leaders

Good formative data not only helps student achievement but also provides a compass to help teachers grow and develop into teacher leaders. Analyzing the data for strengths and areas of growth for teachers provides a needs assessment for teachers who might benefit from professional development around particular content strands. The data also leads to the person or persons who should deliver this professional development. This becomes the groundwork for developing teachers into leaders.

Asking teachers to reflect on their practice, help one another perfect their craft, and add to their pedagogical skills affirms teachers and builds a climate of trust and collaboration. Using data in this way is like the story of the college president who was asked by the construction crew where he wanted the sidewalks for the new building that had just been finished.

> The president said, "I want you to wait a year."
>
> "Wait a year?" the construction foreman asked.
>
> "Yes, wait a year. After that time, it will become clear where to put the sidewalks."
>
> A year passed and the construction crew came back. Carved into the grass were clear paths the students had worn that were the best routes for them to walk.
>
> "Put your sidewalks there." The college president pointed out the obvious.

Similar to these paths, the data will lead to teacher/leaders based upon the skills they have to offer and the paths they choose to go down. The job of the school leader is to foster these teacher/leader roles and give those who fit the job the resources and support they need to help other colleagues. Great instructional leadership comes from great instructional skills and strategies in the classroom.

Teachers who demonstrate a skill in organizing data and analysis may be guided to lead these discussions in their grade level or content area teams. Teachers who show expertise in intervention strategies may guide the instructional implication and goal-setting action plan discussions. Distributive leadership is the key to sustaining the SCORE Process and embedding it into the culture. Research defines seven principle actions that foster teacher leadership, and we link them to the SCORE Process (Crowther, Kaagen, Ferguson, & Hann, 2002).

1. Communicate a clear strategic intent: providing teachers with clear goals and cultivating an environment of innovation to meet students' needs will develop through the instructional implication discussions.

2. Incorporate the aspirations and ideas of others: providing collaboration during assessment creation, data discussions, and goal writing will engage teachers to share and inspire one another.

3. Pose difficult-to-answer questions: heightening the professional dialogue around formative instructional practice and asking questions about student performance will provide opportunities to pose questions to teachers and cause reflection and commitment.

4. Make space for individual innovation: encouraging teachers to try new strategies and instructional practice will lead to innovation.

5. Know when to step back: demonstrating trust in teachers to find solutions and reach high expectations will emerge through this process. Don't provide all the answers; leave some questions for teachers to solve together.

6. Create opportunities out of perceived difficulties: presenting the opportunity for reflection, growth, and collaboration when poor data comes in will lead to solutions.

7. Build on achievements to create a culture of success: finding the success and highlighting it throughout the process will help celebrate the success. Remember that great oak trees grow from little acorns.

We were always amazed after traveling to the same district for a couple of years at how these teacher/leaders naturally presented themselves. In one district, a math teacher who had been a statistics major in college disseminated the data for the entire staff, creating helpful spreadsheets to organize it. In another district, the librarian created teacher and student files that organized the data for parents to be able to better understand. In another district, a language arts teacher took over the school leader position in the formative assessment process. She believed in what the school was trying to do, and the superintendent recognized this, giving her a stipend and cutting back her teaching schedule so she could work on it.

Modeling the effective use of data will be an everyday occurrence when using formative assessment practices effectively. Data will be used to guide all decisions throughout the school. It is used when the teachers use the assessment blueprints in creating the assessments. It is used when the assessments have been graded and data analysis occurs with teachers and students. It is used when the school leader identifies teacher/leaders to guide the SCORE Process, and it is used to form the culture and climate of success throughout the school.

Answer to Formative Assessment Question #7: What are efficient ways to organize data so it can be put to meaningful use?

Having data that can be used for both student and teacher improvement is the entire purpose of the SCORE Process. One way to ensure that the data can be analyzed properly is to organize it in a purposeful manner. Breaking it down by student, question, type of question, and CCSS, as well as those who do not master a certain aspect, are ways to organize that allow teachers to search for patterns.

Answer to Formative Assessment Question #8: Once the data is organized, what are ways to analyze it to improve student achievement?

Once you have the data organized, it is important for the school leader to show the staff ways the data can be looked at and how to look for patterns. Teachers will be like detectives, looking for clues as to why a student was successful with certain aspects and not so successful with others. Identifying these patterns allows teachers to know what needs to be adapted in the classroom to bring about better student achievement. These changes make for better teaching and improved teachers. Teachers can then use a similar method with their students so that they can look at their own data and figure out ways to improve their achievement, empowering them in the process.

chapter six

Transforming the School

*An organization that does not change
and evolve does not improve* (Anthony Muhammad, 2009).

There is a big difference between change and transformation. Changing the school schedule for testing, adjusting some courses for students to help them prepare, or shifting teacher assignments to put them in a position of strength—these can be done right now and will certainly elicit change. That does not mean the school has been transformed. Transformation takes a while. Research has shown that real transformation takes between three and five years of consistent practice to permeate the culture and climate of a school.

The SCORE Process leads to transformation of a school with consistent and sustained practice across several years. Indicators that this transformation is occurring will be when teachers just naturally ask higher-level questions in their classrooms because they have been writing them for their formative assessments. Another indicator is that students feel as comfortable writing the constructed responses as they do the multiple-choice answers because they have been doing them in class for everyday practice. Or the common formative assessments the students have been taking become part of a routine that they know is going to happen every nine weeks or so, and the energy toward this process is positive rather than filled with dread.

The transformation becomes embedded into the DNA of the school, although it does not happen right before your eyes. The transformation will be most evident when high-stakes test results come back from the state. Success breeds success. The improvement of student achievement will be a part of the transformation as will the increased confidence and ability of the teaching staff. However, the school leader will want to continue making changes for the better concerning the SCORE Process.

Celebrate Your Success

Sometimes school leaders are quick to point out where students and teachers did not do well or where improvements need to be made, but they need to give equal focus to success. After each assessment, school leaders should let students and teachers know that doing well is valued. That also helps students and teachers see the value in the SCORE Process and that the school and administration appreciate their efforts. This helps establish a positive attitude for the next round of formative assessments and begins to transform the environment.

We encourage school leaders to celebrate in a simple or a grand manner. An example of a grand celebration would be having a school assembly where top, most improved, and steadiest students receive certificates for their achievements—almost like a pep rally for academics. Inviting parents of the recipients scaffolds the success to home and helps build the family-school connection. Another form of celebrating success may come in the morning announcements where names of high achievers are given recognition.

Each teacher may decide how to celebrate success in his or her own classroom. Some suggestions would be displaying in the classroom a top-five achievement guide. A teacher may display the student profile, minus names to prevent any embarrassment, highlighting those students with high scores. Teachers may also display the item analysis and trumpet those CCSS the students mastered at a high percentage. Displaying these graphs where students see their success and others see themselves compared supports students' setting higher goals to aim for during the next round of formative assessments.

However the school decides to celebrate, as individual teachers or as a collective school, applauding good news improves student and teacher attitudes toward the assessments as well as demonstrates that the data drives the transformation of the school.

Revising the Process

An important aspect of the SCORE Process is to tweak and refine the process, remembering that nothing is written in stone. This ranges from pacing guides to formative assessments to teachers' lesson plans. Everything is a piece of clay that needs to be shaped and altered to make sure it is the best it can be. This brings us to step seven in the SCORE Process, revising (Figure 6.1).

Figure 6.1 Step Seven in the SCORE Process

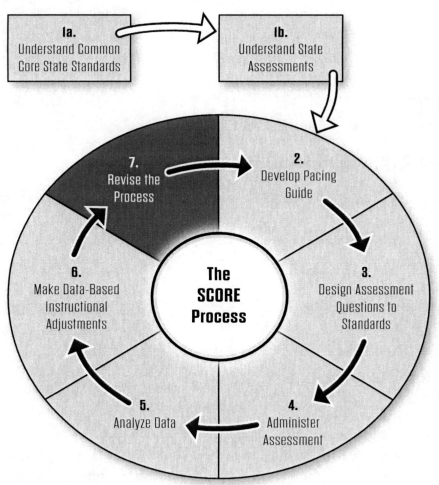

In using the data to make instructional implications and refinements, the school leader should use the same data to revise and edit pacing guides and/or assessment items.

Pacing Guides

The pacing guide will need to be revisited. Questions that guide the revision of the pacing guide might include the following:

- Was the group able to teach the required CCSS in a manner with which they felt comfortable?

- Did the students master the CCSS?

- Is the mastery of the CCSS backed up with data? If not, certain standards might have to be shuffled, reassessed, or taught in a different manner.

- Are the CCSS in logical sequence?

Revision of the pacing guide is a short process, but addressing and responding to teacher concerns that are supported in the data is important.

Revisiting Assessments

Immediately after giving the first assessment and disseminating the data, teachers should have revising and editing discussions. First, using the group's item analysis data, teachers should revisit every question students had difficulty with (only thirty percent of students demonstrated success) and consider revising questions that were answered with much success (more than ninety percent of students demonstrated success). Going through each test item provides a chance to discuss several factors:

- Was the test item written as clearly as it needs to be?

- Does it align with the CCSS?

- Does it align with how the teachers taught the CCSS?

When revising test items students were not successful on, teachers should be careful not to make the questions easier. That would certainly improve results but may not measure what the standard intends. It means determining that the skill the pacing guide aims to measure is truly being measured. If the item does align and is clearly written, this becomes an instructional implication for the future. An example of an instructional issue and not an item issue is if a test item had students retelling a selection through extended response and students had to write a beginning, middle, middle, end event, but the students had never seen the graphic organizer on the assessment before and were not familiar with the middle, middle parts.

Conversely, when revising a question students were very successful on, teachers should make sure the question aligns with the standard and the level of mastery the standard is seeking. If it does, teachers should look at other possible problems, such as a multiple-choice question with distractors that are easy to eliminate or a constructed-response question that elicits an answer that is too broad.

Some teachers might want to be done with the formative assessment and put it away until next year to revise. The problem with waiting is that the issues that were fresh in the group's minds become dull with time and may be forgotten. This is where the Post-Assessment Revision Form, found in the Principal's Office (page 111), can be used after giving each assessment to help in the revision process.

Although getting feedback from the staff is important, equally important or maybe even more so is getting the reaction of the students. The school leader should consider informally or formally surveying the students to see what they liked and did not like. This can be done by having teachers ask general questions of their students or by having the students fill out formal surveys to gather feedback. Some of this information may be useful in creating a more successful testing environment the next time. Say, for instance, one of the assessment days was interrupted with a scheduled fire drill. Students might mention this on the survey and when the teacher goes back and looks at the data, sure enough students struggled with that particular assessment. The school leader should schedule the assessment when there are no scheduled fire drills (you would think this is a no-brainer, but you would be surprised). A sample of a questionnaire teachers can give their students following the assessment can be found in the Principal's Office (page 113).

Another way to gather student input is for teachers to go through the assessment with the students and ask them to think about why they answered certain questions in certain ways. This discussion will indicate students' interpretation of the assessment items and provide valuable insight into the revision process.

Revision is not an afterthought in the SCORE Process; it is a vital part that needs to be done correctly in order for the process to be successful. This involves revisiting and revising the pacing guides and modifying and correcting the assessments to be sure they are as valid as possible. It also means going over the testing procedures to be sure everything goes more smoothly with the next round of assessments.

Making the process better includes identifying teacher/leaders and putting them in places where they can best assist the process. Like most things in life, the more a school leader does this, the easier it becomes until it is ingrained in the staff and students, and the building is successfully transformed.

Data-Based Culture and Climate

Underlying the entire formative assessment process is the belief in data-driven instructional decisions. Going through the SCORE Process changes the school and student growth in the content areas. However, to truly transform a school climate and culture, a school leader must use data analysis and decision making at every turn. This means when a teacher asks to go on a field trip or institute a new program, the first thought in the school leader's head needs to be, "What is the basis for this request?" In other words, what data does the teacher have that supports making a decision? Having teachers provide data to support decisions and requests is at the core of the formative assessment process and the key to having a transformational building.

When the school leader models data-based decision making, the teachers see how data-based instruction works at every turn. Using data throughout the school becomes the key to consistent decision making, instructional choices, and growth in teachers and students.

Answer to Formative Assessment Question #9: Using the information gathered from the common formative assessments, how can school leaders be purposeful in the transformation of the building?

Transformation is something school leaders want to occur at the deepest levels of their schools. By making changes, school staff eventually sees transformation. These changes need to be purposeful and backed by data.

Change for change's sake is not what we seek. Every change that is made must be justified by something that the data reflected from the common formative assessments.

Answer to Formative Assessment Question #10: How can school leaders ensure that the common formative assessments measure what they want them to?

A good first step school leaders can take to ensure that the transformation of the school is ongoing is to revise the SCORE Process each time it is used. This guarantees that the common formative assessments measure what is desired, that students learn what is necessary, and that teachers develop into leaders to improve student achievement. Revising the SCORE Process results in the long-term transformation of the building.

chapter seven

Final Words of Advice

Some men give up their designs when they have almost reached the goal; While others, on the contrary, obtain a victory by exerting, at the last moment, more vigorous efforts than ever before (Herodotus, Greek historian).

*B*e patient. Let us repeat this valuable piece of advice: be patient. Keep in mind that school transformation like any transformation, does not happen overnight. It is important as a school leader that you be the rudder for this journey and that no matter how frustrated you become at the process or its slow progression, you are its greatest champion. If your colleagues or students see you losing faith in the process, they will be quick to join you. You are like the flight attendant on an airplane. During times of turbulence or rough weather, if the flight attendant smiles and acts as if it is simply part of the ride, the passengers will be calm and know that everything is going to be all right. If, however, the flight attendant panics or runs up and down the aisle screaming that everyone is going to die, the passengers will follow suit and chaos will ensue. Keep your eyes on the prize throughout the entire SCORE Process. This prize is higher student achievement and development of teachers into data-driven leaders.

It is important to remember that this is a process. Many of the buildings we worked with did not see significant transformation until a couple of years into the SCORE Process. People grumbled every time we walked into their building that we were wasting valuable class time. What made it worthwhile was watching those very same people buy into the process, slowly, but surely. Some of these naysayers became our biggest advocates. The good news is there will be transformation of both teachers and students. There is a tendency in education to jump on the latest trend and ride it until the next flashy trend because the previous one did not work immediately. This ever-revolving carousel prevents any meaningful, long-term transformation from occurring. Stay the course, and the benefits the school will reap will far outweigh the headaches experienced along the way. Watch all stakeholders grow and learn and become the best they can be. Believe us, the journey is well worth the destination.

The Principal's Office

Normally thought of in a negative connotation, the Principal's Office in this book is a place you want to go. It has resources, reproducibles, and other items that will help school leaders through the process of creating common formative assessments for their schools.

Contents

- Explanation of Various Examples of Formative Assessments as provided by the West Virginia Department of Education 84
- Curriculum Pacing Guide 90
- Writing Multiple-Choice Items, provided by University of Indiana Department of Education. 91
- Presentation of Formative Assessment Process to Staff 94
- Testing Tips That Can Be Used for Announcements 100
- Do Not Disturb Sign 101
- Test Directions for Common Formative Assessment 102
- Class Profile Graph Directions. 104
- Blank Class Profile Graph 106
- Classroom Item Analysis Directions 107
- Blank Classroom Item Analysis Graph 108
- Non-Mastery Report Directions 109
- Blank Non-Mastery Report 110
- Post-Assessment Revision Form 111
- Student Questionnaire 113

Explanation of Various Examples of Formative Assessments as provided by the West Virginia Department of Education

http://wvde.state.wv.us/teach21/ExamplesofFormativeAssessment.html

Observations

The more we know about students, the more we can help them. Observations, sometimes called kid watching, can help teachers determine what students do and do not know. There are several instruments and techniques that teachers can use to record useful data about student learning. Here are a few:

Anecdotal Notes: These are short notes written during a lesson as students work in groups or individually, or after the lesson is complete. The teacher should reflect on a specific aspect of the learning (sorts geometric shapes correctly) and make notes on the student's progress toward mastery of that learning target. The teacher can create a form to organize these notes so that they can easily be used for adjusting instruction based on student needs.

Anecdotal Notebook: The teacher may wish to keep a notebook of the individual observation forms or a notebook divided into sections for the individual students. With this method, all of the observations on an individual student are together and can furnish a picture of student learning over time.

Anecdotal Note Cards: The teacher can create a file folder with 5" × 7" note cards for each student. This folder is handy for middle and high school teachers because it provides a convenient way to record observations on students in a variety of classes.

Labels or Sticky Notes: Teachers can carry a clipboard with a sheet of labels or a pad of sticky notes and make observations as they circulate throughout the classroom. After the class, the labels or sticky notes can be placed in the observation notebook in the appropriate student's section.

Whatever the method used to record observations on students' learning, the important thing is to use the data collected to adjust instruction to meet student needs.

Questioning

Asking better questions affords students an opportunity for deeper thinking and provides teachers with significant insight into the degree and depth of student understanding. Questions of this nature engage students in classroom dialogue that expands student learning. Questions should go beyond the typical factual questions requiring recall of facts or numbers. Paul Black, a noted authority on formative assessment, suggests that "more effort has to be spent in framing questions that are worth asking: that is, questions which explore issues that are critical to the development of students' understanding." (Black et al., 2003)

Discussion

Classroom discussions can tell the teacher much about student learning and understanding of basic concepts. The teacher can initiate the discussion by presenting students with an open-ended question. The goal is to build knowledge and develop critical and creative thinking skills. Discussions allow students to increase the breadth and depth of their understanding while discarding erroneous information and expanding and explicating background knowledge (Black and Wiliam 1998; Doherty 2003). By activating students as learning resources for one another there is the possibility of some of the largest gains seen in any educational intervention (Slavin, Hurley and Chamberlain 2003). The teacher can assess student understanding by listening to the student responses and by taking anecdotal notes.

Exit Slips/Admit Slips

Exit Slips are written responses to questions the teacher poses at the end of a lesson or a class to assess student understanding of key concepts. They should take no more than 5 minutes to complete and are taken up as students leave the classroom. The teacher can quickly determine which students have it, which ones need a little help, and which ones are going to require much more instruction on the concept. By assessing the responses on the Exit Slips the teacher can better adjust the instruction in order to accommodate students' needs for the next class.

Admit slips are exactly like Exit Slips, but they are done prior to or at the beginning of the class. Students may be asked to reflect on their understanding of their previous night's homework, or they may reflect on the previous day's lesson if the question required a longer response time. Exit and Admit Slips can be used in all classes to integrate written communication into the content area.

Learning Logs/Response Logs

Learning Logs are used for students' reflections on the material they are learning. This type of journal is in common use among scientists and engineers. In the log, students record the process they go through in learning something new, and any questions they may need to have clarified. This allows students to make connections to what they have learned, set goals, and reflect upon their learning process. The act of writing about thinking helps students become deeper thinkers and better writers. Teachers and students can use Learning Logs during the formative assessment process, as students record what they are learning and the questions they still have, and teachers monitor student progress toward mastery of the learning targets in their log entries and adjust instruction to meet student needs. By reading student logs and delivering descriptive feedback on what the student is doing well and suggestions for improvement, the teacher can make the Learning Log a powerful tool for learning.

Response Logs are a good way to examine student thinking. They are most often connected with response to literature, but they may be used in any content area. They offer students a place to respond personally, to ask questions, to predict, to reflect, to collect vocabulary and to compose their thoughts about text. Teachers may use Response Logs as formative assessment during the learning process.

Graphic Organizers

Graphic organizers are visual models that can assist students in organizing information and communicating clearly and effectively. Students can use graphic organizers to structure their writing, brainstorm ideas, assist in decision making, clarify story structure, help with problem solving, and plan research. These are a few of the more common graphic organizers:

Venn Diagram	KWL Chart
Brainstorming Web	Mind Map
T Chart	Concept Map

Peer/Self Assessments

Peer and self assessment help to create a learning community within the classroom. When students are involved in criteria and goal setting, self evaluation becomes a logical step in the learning process. Students become metacognitive and are more aware of their personal strengths and weaknesses. With peer assessment students begin to see each other as resources for understanding and checking for quality work against previously determined criteria. The teacher can examine the self assessments and the peer assessments and identify students' strengths and weaknesses. "When students are required to think about their own learning, articulate what they understand, and what they still need to learn, achievement improves." (Black and Wiliam 1998)

Practice Presentations

Just as in sports, practice before a classroom presentation is vital. Through practice and peer review, students can improve their presentation skills and the content of the presentation itself. The practice presentation should take place a few days before the final presentation due date. Students run through their presentations with the audience, their peers, evaluating the performance based on the previously established rubric criteria. An easy way for students to furnish feedback is through a T Chart. Students use the left column of the chart to comment on the positive aspects of the presentation, and they use the right columns to suggest changes that the presenter might make to improve the quality of the presentation. By listening to both the practice and final presentations the teacher can easily gauge the level of student understanding of critical concepts and adjust instruction to address any misconceptions.

Visual Representations

There are several forms of visual representation, or nonlinguistic representation, but one that offers assessment data for the teacher is the use of drawing. Graphic organizers can be used as visual representations of concepts in the content areas. Many of the graphic organizers contain a section where the student is expected to illustrate his/her idea of the concept. The Mind Map requires that students use drawings, photos or pictures from a magazine to represent a specific concept. The Verbal and Visual Word Association asks students to illustrate a vocabulary term. Both of these offer the teacher a quick way of assessing student depth of understanding regarding a specific concept and the ability to adjust instruction immediately to address student needs.

86

Kinesthetic Assessments

These examples of the formative assessment process require students to incorporate movement to demonstrate their understanding of a topic or concept. Although usually connected with the Arts (dance, playing a musical piece) or physical education (dribbling a basketball, serving a volleyball), kinesthetic assessments can be used in the core content classrooms to furnish teachers with insight into their students' understandings and misconceptions concerning a concept. Kinesthetic assessments are a good way to add movement in the classroom and allow teachers to determine the depth of student learning to inform their instructional decisions.

Individual Whiteboards

Individual slates or whiteboards are a great way to hold all students in the class accountable for the work. They actively involve students in the learning and are a terrific tool in the formative assessment process because they give the teacher immediate information about student learning. When students complete their work and hold their whiteboard up, the teacher can quickly determine who is understanding and who needs help and adjust his/her instruction accordingly.

Laundry Day

Laundry Day is a strategy in the formative assessment process mentioned by Cassandra Erkens in her article entitled "Scenarios on the Use of Formative Classroom Assessment" (2007). This is a strategy where students evaluate their own learning in preparation for a chapter or unit test. They group themselves in the classroom around four different kinds of laundry detergent: Tide, Gain, Bold and Cheer. In their chosen corner they will work on activities to enrich or improve their understanding of the required content. The teacher can readily assess the students' level of understanding of the basic concepts covered in the unit or chapter. The teacher provides support as needed, as well as help being provided by students who are sure they have mastered the content. None of the work generated during this time counts as a grade, but students are scaffolded to increase their chances of success on the upcoming test.

Four Corners

Four Corners is a quick strategy that can be used effectively in the formative assessment process for gauging student understanding. It can engage students in conversations about controversial topics. The four corners of the classroom can be labeled as Strongly Agree, Agree, Disagree, and Strongly Disagree. Present students with a statement, like "All students should wear uniforms to school," and have them move to the corner that expresses their opinion. Students could then discuss why they feel the way they do. The teacher can listen to student discussions and determine who has information to support their opinion and who does not. Another way to use Four Corners is associated with multiple choice quizzes. Label the corners of the classroom as A, B, C and D. Students respond to a teacher-created question by choosing the answer they feel is correct. They must be able to give a reason for their answer.

Constructive Quizzes

Periodic quizzes can be used during the formative assessment process to monitor student learning and adjust instruction during a lesson or unit. Constructive quizzes will not only furnish teachers with feedback on their students, but they serve to help students evaluate their own learning. By using quizzes to furnish students with immediate feedback, the teacher can quickly determine the status of each student in relation to the learning targets, and students can learn more during the discussions that immediately follow the quizzes, instead of having to wait until the next day to see the results of the assessment in the form of a meaningless grade on the top of a paper. The teacher should use the results of these quizzes to adjust instruction immediately based on student outcomes.

Think-Pair-Share

Think-Pair-Share (Lyman, 1981) is a summarization strategy that can be used in any content area before, during, and after a lesson. The activity involves three basic steps. During the "think" stage, the teacher tells students to ponder a question or problem. This allows for wait time and helps students control the urge to impulsively shout out the first answer that comes to mind. Next, individuals are paired up and discuss their answer or solution to the problem. During these steps students may wish to revise or alter their original ideas. Finally, students are called upon to share with the rest of the class. There is also a Think-Pair-Square-Share. In this strategy, partners discuss answers with another pair before sharing with the class. This activity ensures that all students are interacting with the information. Teachers can use this activity in the formative assessment process as they walk about the room listening to student conversations. It is important that the teacher collect the data not just by observation, but in anecdotal notes or check sheets.

Appointment Clock

The Appointment Clock is a simple strategy in the formative assessment process that can be embedded within a lesson. The teacher directs students to find the people with whom to schedule appointments at the quarter hour, the half hour, and the 45-minute mark. The teacher begins the lesson and provides information to move students to higher-order thinking. The teacher determines the stopping point and asks students to meet with their quarter hour appointment to discuss their thinking about a couple of questions the teacher has posed. The teacher walks around and listens to the conversations taking place between partners, noting any misconceptions or misunderstandings. The teacher uses this information to adjust instruction by redirecting the next segment of the lesson. Students meet with their half hour appointment and the teacher conducts the same informal observation and adjusts the third section of the lesson. Students continue this process until the lesson is complete. By structuring a lesson in this manner, the teacher is able to determine the current level of understanding for the class and for individual students, and make immediate adjustments to instruction to assist students in their learning.

As I See It

As I See It is a formative assessment technique that focuses students' thinking on their own knowledge or opinions.

1. Determine the number of rows you would like on the template. Create and enter in the sentence stems on the template.

    Examples of types of sentence stems

    1. Personal Statements

        a. When I read this, I imagine that …

        b. I was most impacted by …

    2. Explanatory Statements

        a. The angle changes because …

    3. Prediction Statements

        a. Based on the data, I predict …

    4. Confusion Declarations

        a. After today, I am still confused about …

2. Make and distribute enough copies for each student.

3. Ask students to express their knowledge or opinions using the stems.

4. Discuss what students have discovered about their own opinions or levels of knowledge.

Curriculum Pacing Guide

District _____ *Grade Level* _____ *Subject Area* _____

Grading Period 1	Grading Period 2	Grading Period 3	Grading Period 4

Writing Multiple-Choice Items, as provided by University of Indiana Department of Education (2011)

The challenge is to write questions that test a significant concept, that are unambiguous, and that don't give test-wise students an advantage.

1. The stem should fully state the problem and all qualifications. To make sure that the stem presents a problem, always include a verb in the statement.

2. Concentrate on writing items that measure students' ability to comprehend, apply, analyze, and evaluate as well as recall.

3. Include words in the stem that would otherwise be repeated in each option. Following this guideline not only saves time for the typist but also saves reading time for the student.

   Poor: Sociobiology can be defined as

   a. the scientific study of humans and their relationships within the environment.

   b. the scientific study of animal societies and communication.

   c. the scientific study of plants and their reproductive processes.

   d. the scientific study of the number of species in existence.

   Better: Sociobiology can be defined as the scientific study of

   a. humans and their relationships within the environment.

   b. animal societies and communication.

   c. plants and their reproductive processes.

   d. the number of species in existence.

4. Eliminate excessive wording and irrelevant information in the stem.

5. Make sure there is only one correct or best response.

   Poor: The function of the hypothesis in a research study is to provide

   a. tentative explanation of phenomena.

   b. proven explanation of phenomena.

   c. framework for interpretation of the findings.

   d. direction for the research.

   There is no single or best answer; options a, c, and d are correct. The options need to be reworded so that only one is clearly best or correct. Or one could change the stem: According to the lecture (or the text), the most important function of the hypothesis is. ...

6. Provide a minimum of three, but not more than five, plausible and attractive options for each item. A good procedure is to think of errors that students are likely to make and use these as distractors.

Poor: The recent (1989) research suggesting that controlled nuclear-fusion could be affected in a laboratory experiment at room temperature was conducted by

a. Watson and Crick.

b. Pons and Fleischmann.

c. Koch and Jenner.

d. Fermi and Bohr.

While the first two options are plausible, the last two are not. The latter should be replaced by the names of contemporary scientists.

7. Make all the options for an item approximately homogeneous in content, form, and grammatical structure. Increasing the homogeneity of the content among the options can increase the difficulty of an item. (Difficulty of a test should not be based on inclusion of obscure content.)

8. Avoid the use of the all-of-the-above and none-of-the-above options. The problem with "all of the above" as an option is that it makes the item too easy. If students can recognize at least one incorrect option, they can eliminate "all of the above" as a viable option. On the other hand, if they can recognize at least two correct options, then they know that "all of the above" is the correct answer. Furthermore, research shows that when "all of the above" is used as a distractor, it is too often the correct response. Students are quick to pick up on this clue.

"None of the above" should be used only when absolute standards of correctness can be applied, such as in math, grammar, spelling, geography, historical dates, and so on. Otherwise, students can often argue about the correctness of one of the other options.

9. Avoid verbal associations between the stem and the correct option; e.g., the same reference word should not appear in the stem and an option. Also make sure that the options are grammatically consistent with the stem.

Poor: The correlation coefficient found by correlating students' scores on a classroom math test with their scores on a standardized math test is called a

a. validity coefficient.

b. index of reliability.

c. equivalence coefficient.

d. internal consistency coefficient.

Option (a) is the only one that is grammatically consistent with the stem. It could be correctly selected without knowing anything about the content. One should change the "a" in the stem to "a(n)."

10. Avoid making the correct answer markedly longer or shorter than the other options.

11. If there is a logical sequence in which the alternatives can be arranged (alphabetical if a single word, in order of magnitude if numerals, in temporal sequence, or by length of response), use that sequence.

12. Use negatively stated stems sparingly. When used, call attention to the negative word by underlining and/or capitalizing.

13. Randomly distribute the correct response among the alternative positions throughout the test. That is, have approximately the same proportion of As, Bs, Cs, Ds, and Es as the correct response.

14. Watch for specific determiners such as "all," "always," and "never," which are more likely to be in incorrect options. Others like "usually" and "sometimes," are more likely to be in the keyed response.

15. Multiple-choice items should be independent. That is, an answer to one question should not depend on the answer to another question.

16. Avoid the use of language that your students won't understand. For example (unless it's a French test), use "cause" instead of "raison d'être" in the question.

17. State items so there can be only one interpretation of their meaning.

Poor: Which one of the following is the best source of heat for home use?

a. Gas

b. Electricity

c. Oil

d. Geothermal

The answer depends on how the question is interpreted. Does the question ask about the best source economically, in terms of cleanness, in terms of efficiency, or just what? Also the correct answer might depend on what part of the world we're asking about.

Better: The most economical source of heat in the midwestern U.S. is

a. gas.

b. electricity.

c. oil.

d. geothermal.

Formative Assessment . . . an Instructional Process

"We cannot solve problems with the same thinking we used when creating the problems"

Albert Einstein

Why Formative Assessment ???

- Formative Assessments will help you find out exactly where your students fall with regard to the Academic Content Standards, and therefore better prepare them for the high-stakes test.

- Formative Assessments will give you information ahead of time, instead of waiting until the results of the high-stakes tests come out.

- It's what is best for kids.

Begin with the end in mind . . .

"Unlike exams, whose purpose it to assign grades based on students' understanding, the purpose of assessment is to determine the impact of instruction on improving student learning."

M. Sunberg

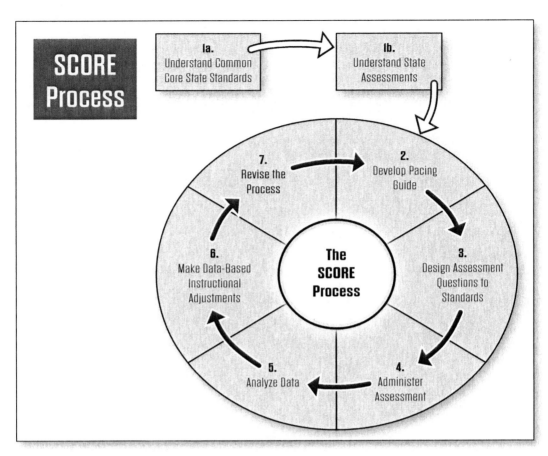

It is assessment which helps us
distinguish between teaching and learning.

Research on Effects of Short-Cycled Assessments

- Black and Wiliam (1998)   .5 to 1.5
- Rodriguez (2004)   .5 to 1.8

- Largest gains for low achievers

Four Things the SCORE Process Can Do For You——Otherwise Known as the "Four Es"

- Give planned and purposeful <u>exposure</u> to the benchmarks, indicators, and formats.

- Develop <u>expertise</u> in each teacher's ability to ask higher level questions, base instructional decisions for delivery on performance data, and collaborate for curricular direction across grade levels.

- Build resilience and <u>endurance</u> for each student to be able to (1) sit through the test and (2) work through difficult quesstions.

- To <u>empower</u> students and their parents to become responsible decision makers for learning.

Ensuring Quality

- Validity

  - ☐ Can these scores be used to describe what students have learned?

  - ☐ Can the scores be used to diagnose student strengths and weaknesses?

  - ☐ Can you make predictions based on the data for the achievement or state tests?

Interpretation

- Our tests communicate our goals

  - ☐ What is important?

  - ☐ What deserves focus?

  - ☐ What we expect as good performance?

Interpretation

"When instruction and assessment are linked to a common set of learning goals, the assessment can be used to improve instruction." Herman, et al. (2009)

Interpretation

"It is now generally accepted that multiple assessment measures are required to adequately gauge student learning."

M. Sunberg

Testing Tips That Can Be Used on Announcements

- Read each passage and accompanying questions.

- Read and pay careful attention to all directions.

- Read every possible answer—the best one could be last.

- Read and respond to items one at a time rather than thinking about the whole test.

- Reread, when necessary, the parts of a passage needed for selecting the correct answer.

- Don't expect to find a pattern in the positions of the correct answers.

- Don't make uneducated guesses. Try to get the correct answer by reasoning and eliminating wrong answers.

- Decide exactly what the question is asking; one response is clearly best.

- Don't spend too much time on any one question.

- Skip difficult questions until all other questions have been answered. On scrap paper, keep a record of the unanswered items to return to if time permits.

- Make sure to record the answer in the correct place on the answer sheet.

- Change an answer only if you are sure the first one you picked was wrong. Be sure to completely erase changed answers.

- Work as rapidly as possible with accuracy.

- After completing the test, use any remaining time to check your answers.

- Keep a good attitude. Think positively!

TESTING

DO NOT

DISTURB

Test Directions for Common Formative Assessment

Estimated Time: _____

Materials needed:

1. Pass out the short-cycle assessment to students, and instruct them to write their names in the space provided. Distribute #2 pencils to the students who need them.

2. Say to the students:

You are now going to start your short-cycle assessment for (subject) _____.
Please turn to the beginning of your assessment. (Pause.) In this session, you will answer (number of) _____ questions. Some of the questions may be hard for you to answer, but it is important that you do your best. If you are not sure of the answer to a question, you should make your best guess. Choose the best answer for each multiple-choice question, and plan your written answers so they fit in the answer spaces in your Student Answer Booklet. Do not mark your answers in the Question Booklet. Instead, mark your answers for this session in your Student Answer Booklet.

Only what you write in the answer spaces in your Student Answer Booklet will be scored. Some questions have more than one part. Try to answer all the parts. If you are asked to explain or show how you know, be sure to do so. Does anyone have any questions? (Answer any questions the students have about the directions.)

3. Say to the students:

It will probably take you about _____ minutes to answer the questions in this session of the test, but you can have more time if you need it.
When you are finished with all the questions, you may review your answers.

If you get stuck on a word, I can read the word to you. I cannot read numbers, mathematics symbols, or a whole question to you. If you want help reading a word, raise your hand. (Pronounce the word to students who asked for assistance. Do not define the word or help the students in any other way.) Are there any questions? (Answer any questions the students have about the directions.) When you finish, please sit quietly and read until everyone is finished. You may begin.

Directions to Read to the Student

Today you will be taking the formative assessment. This is an indicator of how well you understand the material we have covered over the last grading period.

Different types of questions appear on this test: multiple choice, constructed response, and _____ (choose and add any that apply to your state).

All your answers must be marked or written on your answer sheet.

There are several important things to remember:

1. You may look at any part of the test as often as necessary.

2. Read each question carefully. Think about what is being asked. If a graph or another diagram goes with the question, read it carefully to help you answer the question. Then choose or write the answer that you think is best on your answer sheet.

3. When you are asked to draw or write your answers, draw or write neatly and clearly in the boxes provided.

4. When you are asked to select an answer, make sure you fill in the circle next to the answer on your answer sheet. Mark only one answer.

5. If you do not know the answer to a question, skip it and go on. If you have time, remember to return and complete the question.

6. If you finish the test early, you may check over your work. When you are finished and your test booklet and answer sheet have been collected, sit quietly until the time is up. (Other choices may appear here, such as "take out your silent work.")

7. Write or mark your answers directly on your answer sheet. You may not use scratch paper. Use your test sheet to work out problems.

8. You may use the calculator that is provided, if applicable.

Class Profile Graph Directions

How to use:

- Insert the student names in the provided space at the bottom of the graph.

- Draw a vertical line for the percentage score for each student, coloring it in to create a bar graph.

- Use a black marker and draw a horizontal line at the level you consider proficient. (Many use a 75% line, however, you can choose to make that higher or lower.)

- Using a purple marker, draw a horizontal line at the percentage that is your class average. To calculate the class average, add all the percentages together, and divide that number by the number of students who took the assessment. Now, compare the black line and the purple line. This shows the passage rate that you want to achieve and the actual passage rate of your class.

- Using a blue marker, draw a horizontal line at the percentage that is your upper curve line. To calculate this you need to find the standard deviation. To find the standard deviation you take each student's score and subtract it from the mean. For example, if the student scores are

$$64, 32, 56, 89, 91, 55$$

and the mean is 65, then you would subtract:

$$64 - 65 = -1$$
$$32 - 65 = -33$$
$$56 - 65 = -9$$
$$89 - 65 = +24$$
$$91 - 65 = +26$$
$$55 - 65 = -10$$

Next, you square each deficiency:

$$-1 \times -1 = 1$$
$$-33 \times -33 = 1,089$$
$$-9 \times -9 = 81$$
$$+24 \times +24 = 576$$
$$+26 \times +26 = 676$$
$$-10 \times -10 = 100$$

Next, take these results and add them together. It will look like this:

1

1,089

81

576

676

+100

2,523

Now, divide that sum by the number of scores minus 1. So looking at our work above, that would be 2,523 divided by 5, which rounds up to 505.

The last thing you do is take the square root of this number. That is the standard deviation. In this case, the square root of 505 is 22. If you draw a blue line 22 points above your mean of 65 then your upper curve line is 87.

- Use a red marker and draw a horizontal line at the percentage that is your lower curve line. To calculate this use your standard deviation from your upper curve line, which in the case above was 22, and draw your red line 22 points below the mean of 65 which would place it at 43. Once you have your upper and lower curve lines using a standard deviation of 1, you should understand that statistically speaking, approximately 68% of your students fall within the upper and lower curve. Any scores outside of this band, whether above or below, are considered to be statistically different from the rest of the scores. This is where you look to remediate or enrich. Also, look at the number of students who are clustered right around the 75% line. These are your "bubble" students.

Blank Class Profile Graph

Teacher: _____ Grade: _____ Assessment: _____

	100%	95%	90%	85%	80%	75%	70%	65%	60%	55%	50%	45%	40%	35%	30%	25%	20%	15%	10%	5%	
																					Student Name

Classroom Item Analysis Directions

■ How to use:

☐ Indicate the question number, along with the standard, at the bottom of the graph along the X axis, and the percentages 0–100 on the Y axis.

☐ Score the possible points for a particular question.

● In other words, if you have twenty-five students taking the assessment and the question is worth one point, there are twenty-five possible points.

● Similarly, if there are twenty-five students and the question is worth four points, possible points would be $25 \times 4 = 100$ points.

☐ Indicate the actual points the class earned.

● In other words if twenty-one of the twenty-five students got the one-point question correct, it is twenty-one actual points.

☐ To get the % mastered, divide the number of actual points by possible points.

● $21 \div 25 = .84$, or 84%

☐ Color in the bar graph according to the percent mastered.

☐ This gives you an indication of how the class performed overall on each question, as well as classroom successes and gaps.

Blank Classroom Item Analysis

Teacher: _____   Grade: ____   Assessment: _____

Question #	1	2	3	4	5	6	7	8	9	10	11	12	13	14	15	16	17	18	19	20	21	22	23	24	25
Standard																									
100%																									
50%																									
0%																									
Actual points																									
Possible points																									
% mastered																									

Non-Mastery Report Directions

- ■ How to use:

  - ☐ Go through each question, and write what standard that question assessed in the blank provided, using the coding from the pacing guide.

    - ● Example: <u>Question #1</u>, Standard: M 2-5

  - ☐ In the lines provided, you may write out the standard for a reference to what the standard was covering. You may want to write the descriptor out word for word, or you may want to write a one- or two-word descriptor of it.

    - ● Example: Analyze problem situations involving measurement concepts, select appropriate strategies, and use an organized approach to solve narrative and increasingly complex problems.

  - ☐ In the box provided, write all the names of the students in your class who did not master that particular question.

    - ● Remember, mastery for a constructed-response question means the student gets a seventy-five percent or above.

      - ○ Example: three points out of four is mastery
                    two points out of four is non-mastery

      - ○ Example: two points out of two is mastery
                    one point out of two is non-mastery

  - ☐ Go through all the questions, placing the names of the students who did not master the question in the appropriate boxes.

  - ☐ This list gives you an indication of how you can group students in your class if you need to go back and reteach a standard. This also informs you which standard(s) you will need to reteach to the entire class, or if you need to go further into depth on a certain standard.

Non-Mastery Report

Question #_____, Standard _____

_____

_____

_____

Question #_____, Standard _____

_____

_____

_____

Question #_____, Standard _____

_____

_____

_____

Post-Assessment Revision Form

Teacher's Name: _____ Date: _____

Subject: _____ Assessment: _____

Complete this chart following administration of the assessment. Prior to the data analysis, complete the chart regarding the issues and possible revisions. Following the data analysis, complete the last column of the chart. Use this chart when revising the assessment prior to the next administration.

Item #	Standard	Issue	Possible Revision	Complete Revision?	
				Yes	No

Item #	Standard	Issue	Possible Revision	Complete Revision?	
				Yes	No

Student Questionnaire

1. Did you find the assessment easy? Why or why not?

2. What did you think about the testing schedule?

3. Did you think the classroom setup made it easier or more difficult to concentrate on your assessment?

4. What did you think of the constructed-response questions?

5. What did you think of your teachers' attitudes toward the assessment? Were they encouraging?

6. Did you feel prepared to take the assessment? Did your teachers cover the material you saw on it?

7. Were there any distractions you feel could have been avoided?

8. What could be done to make your testing experience better?

9. What is your overall attitude toward assessments? Why do you think this is?

10. Did you try as hard on this assessment as you do on your regular schoolwork? Explain why.

References

Ainsworth, L., & Viegut, D. (2006). *Common formative assessments: How to connect standards-based instruction and assessment.* Thousand Oaks, CA: Corwin Press.

Black, P., & Wiliam, D. (1998). *Inside the black box: Raising standards through classroom assessment.* London, England: King's College London School of Education.

Classroom Assessment (2012). http://fcit.usf.edu/assessment/basic/basicasi.html, developed by Pinellas School District and the Florida Center for Instructional Technology at USF.

Crowther, F., Kaagen, S. S., Ferguson, M., & Hann, L. (2002). *Developing teacher leaders: How teacher leadership enhances school success.* Thousand Oaks, CA: Corwin Press.

DuFour, R. (1999, February). Help wanted: Principals who can lead professional learning communities. *NASSP Bulletin, 83* (604).

DuFour, R., DuFour, R., Eaker, R., & Many, T. (2010). *Learning by doing: A handbook for professional learning communities at work* (2nd ed.). Bloomington, IN: Solution Tree Press.

Florida Center for Instructional Technology. Classroom Assessment: Basic Concepts: Reliability and Validity. Retrieved from http://fcit.usf.edu/assessment/basic/basicc.html

Foster, D., & Poppers, A. (2009). Using formative assessment to drive learning—The Silicon Valley mathematics initiative: A twelve-year research and development project. The Noyce Foundation.

Glencoe/McGraw Hill (2005, January). Education up close: Writing effective tests: a guide for teachers. Retrieved from http://www.glencoe.com/sec/teaching-today/educationupclose.phtml/40

Hawken, P. (2010). *The ecology of commerce: A declaration of sustainability.* New York, NY: HarperCollins.

Lang, S., Stanley, T., & Moore, B. (2008). *Short-cycle assessment: Improving student achievement through formative assessment.* Larchmont, NY: Eye On Education.

Marshall, J. M. (2005, July). Formative assessment: Mapping the road to success. A white paper prepared for the *Princeton Review.*

Marzano, R. J. (2003). Using data: Two wrongs and a right. *Educational Leadership, 60*(5), 56–60.

Marzano, R. J. (2006). *Classroom assessments and grading that work.* Alexandria, VA: Association for Supervision and Curriculum Development.

Miller, Michael J. (2012). Reliability and validity. Western International University.

Moore, B., (2011). *I have the data … now what? Analyzing data and making instructional changes.* Larchmont, NY: Eye On Education.

Moore, B., & Stanley, T. (2009). *Critical thinking and formative assessments: Increasing the rigor in your classroom.* Larchmont, NY: Eye On Education.

Muhamed, Anthony (2009) Transforming school culture: how to overcome staff division. Bloomington, IN: Solution Tree.

Nicol, D. J.; Macfarlane-Dick, D. (2006). Formative assessment and self-regulated learning: A model and seven principles of good practice. *Studies in Higher Education, 31*(2), 199–218.

Popham, W. J. (2008). *Transformative assessment.* Alexandria, VA.: Association for Supervision and Curriculum Development.

Sacks, L. (March 2009). Galileo and interim assessment. Massachusetts Department of Elementary and Secondary Education.

Smith, L. W. (2008). Using formative assessment results to predict student achievement on high stakes testing. (Unpublished doctoral dissertation). Liberty University. Lynchburg, VA

Stanley, T., & Moore, B. (2010). *Formative assessments in a professional learning community.* Larchmont, NY: Eye On Education.

Wiliam, D., & Thompson, M. (2007). Integrating assessment with instruction: What will it take to make it work? In C. A. Dwyer (Ed.), The *future of assessment: Shaping teaching and learning* (pp. 53-82). Mahwah, NJ: Lawrence Erlbaum Associates.

Young, S., & Giebelhaus, C. (2005) Formative assessment and its uses for improving student achievement. STI: Education Data Management Solutions.